24 EASY METAL TEXTURES

WITH NO ROLLING MILL REQUIRED

Bradford M. Smith

24 Easy Metal Textures

With No Rolling Mill Required

Published by Whimsey Wylde
Santa Monica, CA

ISBN-979-8-9873915-0-1

DEDICATION

For whatever artistic abilities I have in jewelry and photography, I give thanks to my Mom. For my underlying belief that a person can accomplish anything they really want to do, I am grateful to my Dad. And for the loving support and confidence I have to begin every day, I am blessed to have the best wife and daughters any guy could ever imagine.

- Love you all.

ALSO BY THE AUTHOR

BENCH TIPS FOR JEWELRY MAKING

MORE BENCH TIPS FOR JEWELRY MAKING

BROOM CASTING FOR CREATIVE JEWELRY

MAKING YOUR OWN DESIGN STAMPS

ACCESSORIES FOR THE FOREDOM AND DREMEL

THE RELUCTANT FARMER OF WHIMSEY HILL

http:// amazon.com/author/bradfordsmith

TABLE OF CONTENTS

PREFACE

1. JEWELRY TEXTURES 1
2. HAMMERED FINISHES 5
3. EMBOSSED TEXTURES 13
4. PUNCHES AND STAMPS 17
5. TEXTURING HAMMERS 23
6. ROTARY BRUSHES 27
7. ROTARY ABRASIVE BITS 29
8. HAMMER HANDPIECE 33
9. MISCELLANEOUS 39

ABOUT THE AUTHOR 42

APPENDIX A - Texturing Materials & Supplies 43

APPENDIX B - Sources For Texturing Tools 45

APPENDIX C - Tips for Working With Steel 47

OTHER BOOKS BY THE AUTHOR 53

PREFACE

I made my first piece of jewelry in high school and my second piece after 30 years in a career of manufacturing research & development.

After retiring, I became interested in rockhounding and started exploring desert locations for minerals and crystals. That led to learning the lapidary processes for cutting and polishing which rekindled my interest in metal fabrication - but this time in silver and gold.

I also discovered my love of teaching, via the classroom, by way of public speaking, and through my series of metalworking books. The three activities allow me to pass along what I've learned to others. It also pleases me so much to see students get excited about creating jewelry, showing it off to friends, and perhaps even starting a part-time business.

In my jewelry, I've always liked the elegance and sharp contrast created by adding areas of texture. This is easily done with equipment like a hydraulic press or rolling mill in the classroom. But I realize that many home-based jewelers lack the space or the budget for equipment like this.

In my teaching I learned a number of simple, alternative processes for creating varied textures, and I'm pleased to be able to collect them in this single volume for those looking to expand their knowledge of jewelry practices and metal arts methods.

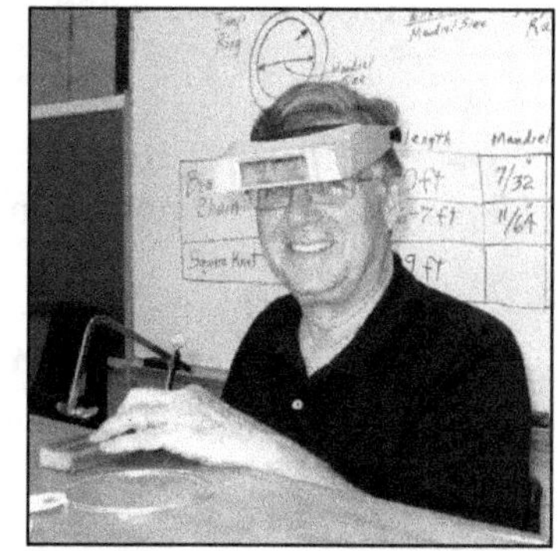

With each technique, I include the tools that will be needed, the procedures for applying the texture, and the options you have for customizing the final look.

Happy hammering!

- Brad

WARNING

Metal Working Tools and Procedures Are Dangerous

Do not attempt procedures described in this book without professional supervision.

All local and industry safety procedures should be followed.

CHAPTER 1

JEWELRY TEXTURES

Texturing adds depth, complexity, and elegance to our jewelry designs. It can be used in an artistic role to provide contrast or visual balance. And it can serve in a functional role to improve grip, to avoid fingerprints left on a mirror surface, or to hide the little nicks of every-day wear.

Adding a mechanical finish to one or more surfaces can enhance the design of your work. First, it will add visual interest and sharpen the contrast between the polished and textured areas. It can also serve a functional role, for instance to provide a non-slip grip or to avoid leaving fingerprints on a piece that is handled frequently.

Surface textures are produced by a large variety of different techniques. Some make use of simple hand tools like hammers, stamps, and punches. Others are applied with tool bits in a Foredom or Dremel. And some require special equipment like a heavy-duty rolling mill or press.

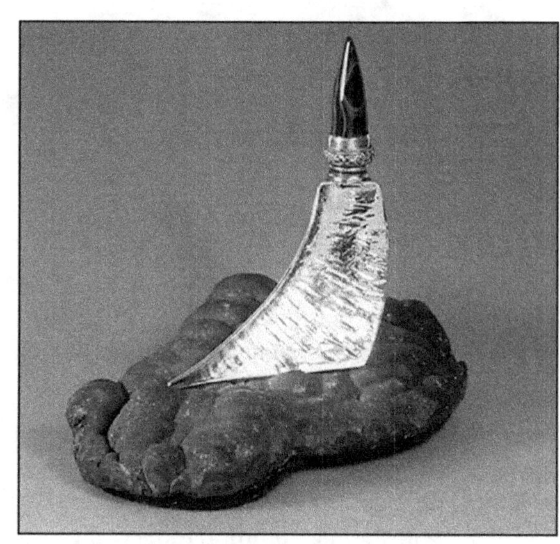

Example of Hammered Texture

Everyone has their favorites, but my aim has always been to show my students as many varieties of a technique as possible. That allows them to choose the best approach for fabricating a design within the limitations of tools they have and equipment available in their shop.

My objective for "Easy Jewelry Textures" is to give examples of the methods I have encountered while making jewelry and teaching classes over many years. With each technique, I'll show the tools that are needed, explain the procedures for applying the texture, and mention options to modify and personalize the final look.

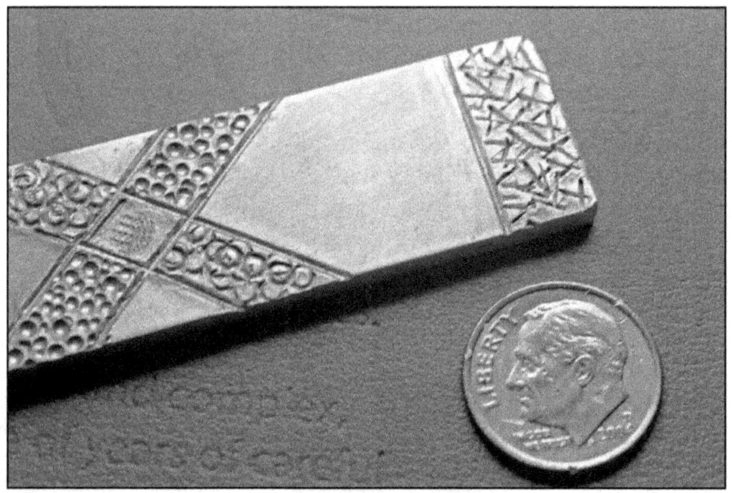

Example of Stamped Textures

None of the techniques included require special equipment any more expensive than a Foredom or Dremel. There are certainly some great ways of using a rolling mill or hydraulic press for texturing sheet, but many jewelry artists just can't justify the cost or lack the necessary space for such heavy equipment.

The chapters that follow describe twenty-four different techniques for adding texture that I have taught in my classes and used in my shop. They generally make use of common tools like hammers, stamps, punches, and tool bits in the flexshaft. And in addition, I'll share how some common tools can be customized with simple modifications to make them very handy for creating useful textures.

Force is Needed

Many textures are applied by pressing a patterning material or a tool into a sheet of metal or the partially completed jewelry workpiece. The amount of force required to get a good impression can be substantial, and in the techniques that follow much of that is supplied by a hammer.

The depth of the texture impression depends on the force of the hammer blow and size of the tool face itself. It's actually the force per square millimeter or square inch.

If the face of the hammer (or the tool that the hammer hits) is small, just a tap of a hammer will do. For instance, a center punch needs only a light tap to make deep divot, but a broader tool like a design stamp might require a large hammer to get the same depth of impression. A familiar example is a hallmark stamp that says "Sterling." Good impressions require a much stronger hit of the hammer than would be used with a center punch.

Tools with a larger area on their face take more force. Think how hard it would be to create a circular impression using the flat face of a ¼ inch diameter steel rod. You would need a two pound hammer and would have to swing it hard enough to be worried about hitting your hand by mistake.

The point is that the amount of force required to press a pattern or texturing tool into a sheet goes up with the area at the tip of the tool. Each texturing tool you select will require a different amount of force to create the same depth of impression.

Some techniques for applying texture will require a large amount of force. The use of these is better suited to flat raw sheet material. Other techniques can be used on partially fabricated surfaces, and a few can even be used on finished soldered work.

Texturing Raw Material

Textures can be applied at various stages of construction. Most however are done in the early stages before much cutting and certainly before any shaping or soldering. It is rather easy at this stage to use any of the texturing procedures and tools mentioned in chapters that follow.

Textures that can be applied to raw materials include:

- hammers with shaped or patterned faces
- steel stamps, punches, or matting tools
- bits or texturing tools in a rotary shaft machine
- hammering or embossing a pattern material

Texturing Partially Finished Work

There are occasions where textures are applied later in the construction sequence. This can be a planned step such as adding a Florentine finish to a ring band, or it can be an unplanned step such as applying a texture to cover a mistake that marred a surface.

Textures that can be applied to partially finished work include:

- tool bits in a rotary shaft machine
- shaped anvil tips in a hammer handpiece
- stamps, punches, or matting tools in limited areas

Texturing Finished Pieces

It's usually quite difficult to apply a lot of force when working on a piece of jewelry that's nearing completion.

Textures that can be applied to finished pieces are fairly limited:

- rotary tool bits in a flexshaft machine
- light textures with a hammer handpiece

CHAPTER 2

HAMMERED FINISHES

Hammering is one the most common ways to apply a surface finish texture without the use of any special equipment. The repetitive hits make up a very pleasing finish - - reminiscent of a seasoned blacksmith using each blow as a way to move and shape the metal.

Visible hammer marks left on a piece give a glimpse into maker's care and skill. The finish shows the work that went into the piece and is valued by those who appreciate good craftsmanship. When hammer hits are closely spaced and carefully positioned, the indentations seem to form a regular pattern.

Many variations are possible with a hammered finish. The detail of each impression is determined by the size, shape, and surface finish of the hammer face. The depth of impressions is influenced by the weight of the hammer head chosen and the force used. It's a combination of these factors that allows a metalsmith to scale a hammered finish up or down to give the desired look to a piece.

There are two bench hammers that are commonly used to produce textured finishes, the ball peen and the cross peen. The tools themselves are staples in every toolbox. They are inexpensive, very effective, easily maintained, and last a lifetime.

Texture 01 - Ball Peen Hammers

When I need a hammer, I usually reach for the ball peen style. It is the most frequently used on my bench. They come in all sizes, but the ones I use most frequently are on the small end of the range. Head sizes from three or four ounces (85-100g) up to eight ounces (200g) match the type of work I do on jewelry-sized projects.

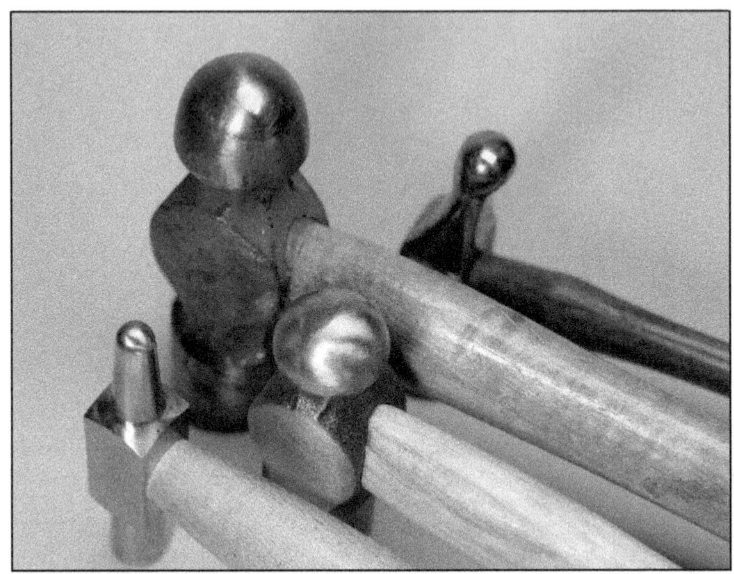

Different Diameter Ball-Peens on Hammers

The biggest difference across ball peen hammers is the size of the ball nose. This determines the coarseness of the hammered finish that is created. The largest ball size shown above is less than an inch (25mm), and the smallest is around a quarter of an inch (6mm).

The only special hammer shown is the Gesswein goldsmiths hammer on the top-right. That's from my mother's old jewelry workbench. It's included here because the 3/8 inch (10mm) ball is a difficult size to find and produces a great hammered finish.

NOTE - These hammers are all rather inexpensive. The quality of steel may not the best but is certainly good enough for applying simple dimpled textures. Useful hammers can be found at yard sales or your favorite local hardware store. Another popular source is online at Amazon.

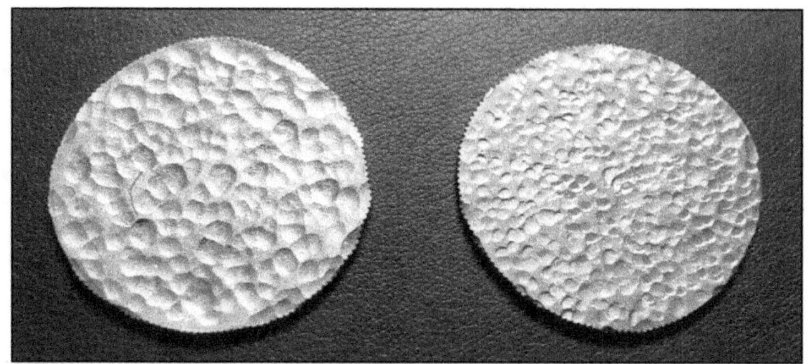
Examples of Ball-Nosed Hammered Finishes

Whenever a hammer is used to put a final finish on a piece of jewelry, it's important that the hammer face and the ball-nosed end are well shaped and polished. See Appendix C for some suggestions on modifying and maintaining your hammers.

Applying a hammered finish to large areas of material is easy, but oftentimes there are obstructions in the way. These could be objects like a bezel or other finished work that's already soldered and must be avoided. In these situations, it's best to make use of a doming ball of roughly the same size as the ball peen that was used. This allows texturing to be completed with precise hits as needed to finish texturing as close to the boundary point as possible.

Texture 02 - Cross Peen Hammers

The cross peen hammer is generally used as a means of moving metal to produce a desired 3-D shape on a workpiece, as in forging or fold-forming. Each hit is linear at a 90-degree angle from the handle.

On a flat metal sheet, the pattern of repetitive hits can be quite beautiful when done with a lighter force than in forging. It leaves a striking finish that adds depth, directionality, and sharp contrast on your work. No heavy hammer heads are needed for producing a cross peen surface finish on common jewelry pieces. Heads in the range of three to four ounces (85-100g) work well for this.

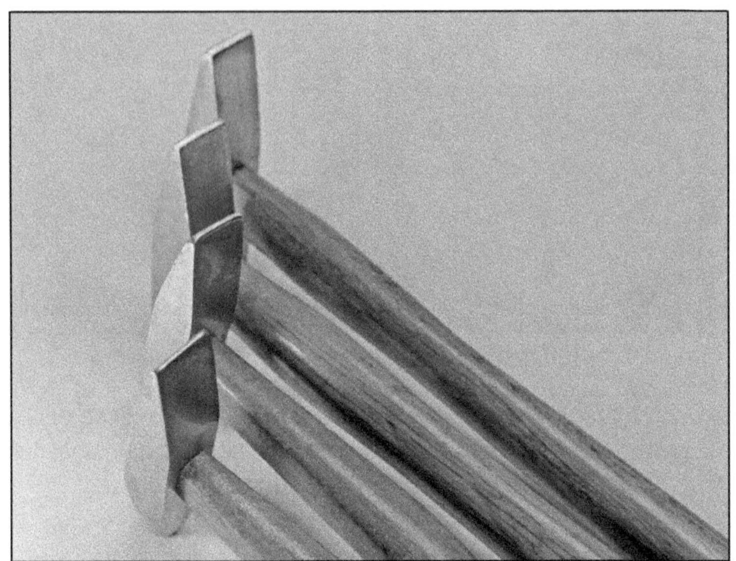
Different Sharpness of Cross-Peens on Hammers

Variations in cross peen surface finish are most heavily governed by the sharpness of the chisel edge and the angular direction of the pattern of hits. Sharp edges, like a dull table knife, will produce a pattern of fine lines that can protrude quite deeply into the sheet. A hammer with more rounded edges will produce a pattern of broader lines that are rather shallow depth on the sheet.

Here are the patterns produced by three hammers with different degrees of roundness on their chisel edges.

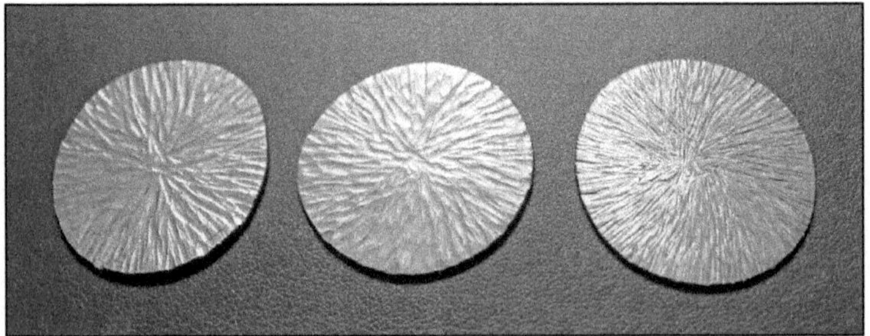
Examples of Cross Peen Hammered Finishes

It's worth taking a little time to experiment with several hammers to see the differences in pattern that can be achieved on your work.

With inexpensive hammers, the edge can often be shaped with a flat file and smoothed with a sanding stick. Better quality hammers are made from steels that are hardened a bit to avoid getting dings on their face. Trying to file one of these will feel like the file is skating across the metal and not biting into it. If this is the case, abrasive tools like grinding wheels will be needed to modify the shape and sandpaper to refine and smooth the chisel edge. Appendix C includes a few tips for doing this.

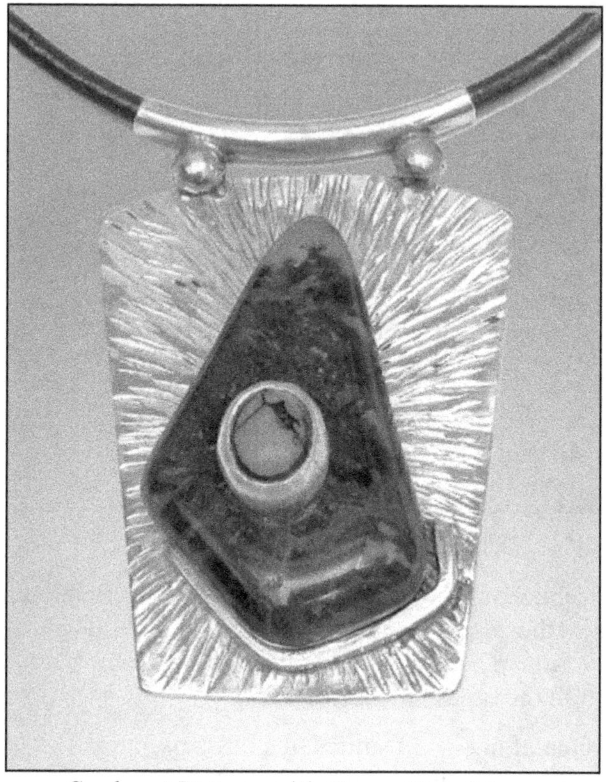

Sunburst Pattern with Cross-Peen Lines

The second factor in applying a cross peen finish is controlling the direction of repetitive hits on the workpiece. This takes a little practice but once learned becomes a favored technique.

One popular pattern is a sunburst. It's a radial pattern of hammered lines emanating from a single center point.

NOTE: Mark the center point with a felt tip pen to serve as a visual aid when hammering sunburst patterns. It helps your eye to keep the chisel edge pointed correctly for each hammer blow.

When the sunburst pattern surrounds an element that is an odd shape, the alignment needs to be planned a little differently. The radial hammer marks will seem a little off if they all point towards a single center point.

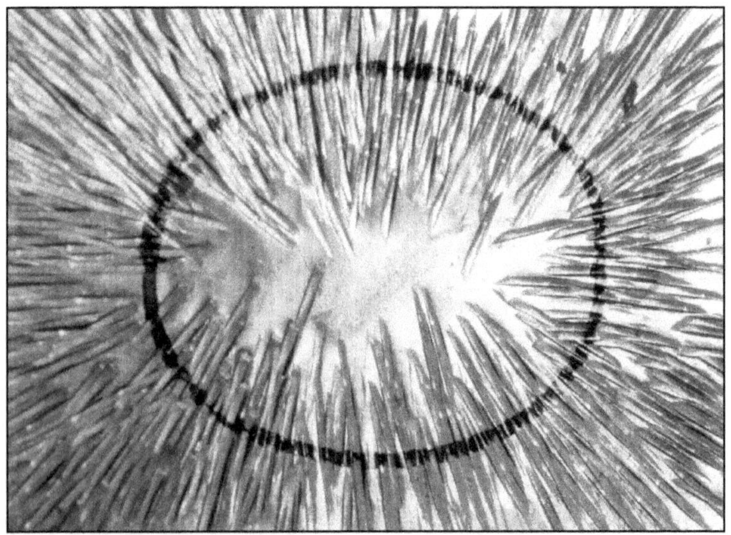

Cross-Peen Lines on an Oval Shape

For oval cabochons, try to position each of the hammered lines so it intersects the edge of the bezel at an angle of 90-degrees. The difference from a centered starburst is only a minor, but it's a detail that is worth the time.

NOTE - One of the nice features of a cross peen texture is that it's easy to correct the pattern if you notice that some of the lines are not at the quite the correct angle. Simply go back over that section of the finish with a new pattern of hits.

Finally, if you wish to extend the cross peen texture into areas that are close to a border or towards some finished work like a soldered bezel, it's best to avoid an accident with the hammer and finish that portion of the texture with a straight-liner stamp that matches the indentations made by the hammer.

It's worth mentioning a bit more about these stamps. Flat-liners are chisel shaped stamps that are used to form straight lines on a workpiece. They are commonly used for detailing an edge or creating a border. They are handy when you need the indentation at a precise location.

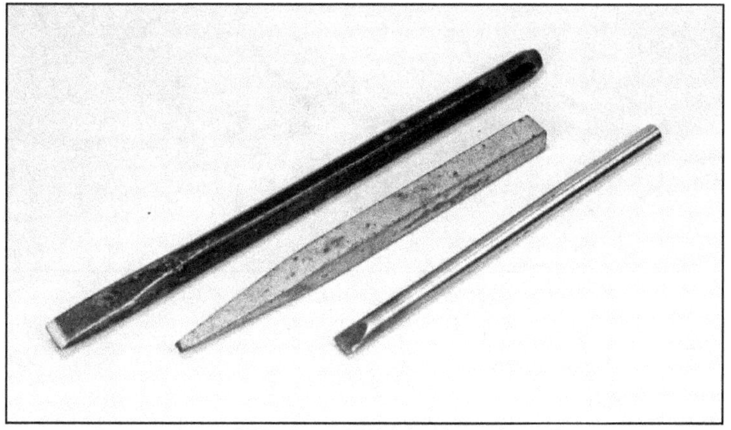

Examples of Various Width Flat Liner Stamps

They come in a variety of widths to produce lines of different lengths from a quarter of an inch (12mm) up to one or two inches (25-50mm).

Straight-liner stamps like this are available commercially from a few sources that are mentioned in Appendix. Similar tools can be found at yard sales and your local hardware store, although they may need a little modification.

Modifying your tools to do the job better or re-purposing a tool for a different job is a skill that serves a jeweler well. If you might be interested doing this, Appendix C includes some pointers.

One example of how easy this might be is a flat-liner made from a section of quality hardened steel from an old file. This one is about ¾ inch (18mm) wide, but the same shape could be made from a needle file.

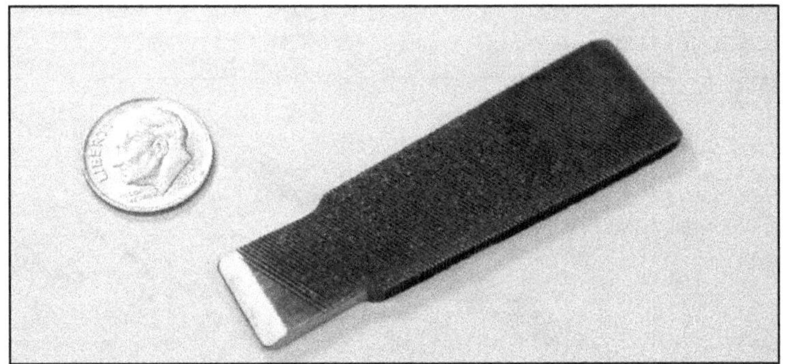

Flat-Liner Made From Section of File

CHAPTER 3

EMBOSSED TEXTURES

The term *embossing* describes the process of pressing a hardened pattern material into annealed metal sheet in order to create a design on its surface, in this case a texture. This takes a lot of pressure is needed, and an easy way to get it is to use a hammer.

For jewelry-sized pieces, there are two embossing techniques that create very useful textures with just a utility hammer, a bench block, and some readily available supplies off your bench. Steel binding wire is used as the pattern material for the first embossed texture, and a piece of very rough sandpaper is used for the second texture.

Both techniques are quick and produce very useful patterns. The pattern material wire or sandpaper can be carried in your toolbox to a class or workshop for use on projects if needed.

Texture 03 - Hammered Wire Nest

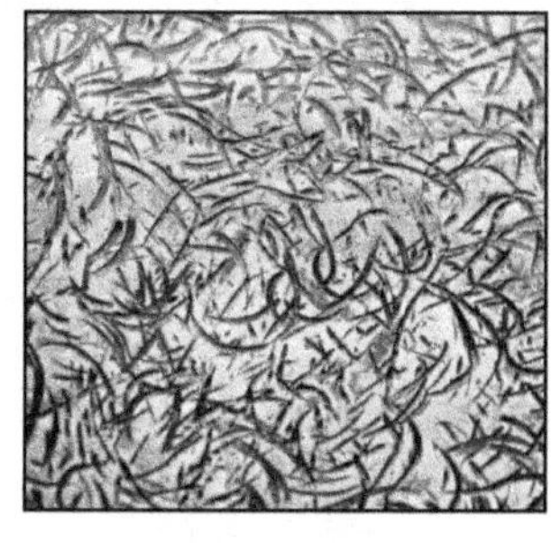

A utility hammer and a length of steel wire is all you need to quickly create a random, curvilinear texture on a sheet of raw material.

Almost any binding wire from the soldering area works. It's readily available from all jewelry supply sources, or you can often find some at a local hardware store. Ask for wire to hang picture frames and then test with a magnet to be sure it is steel.

Copper wire will work in a pinch but has limitations. It will flatten rather quickly under the hammering, and this causes wider lines.

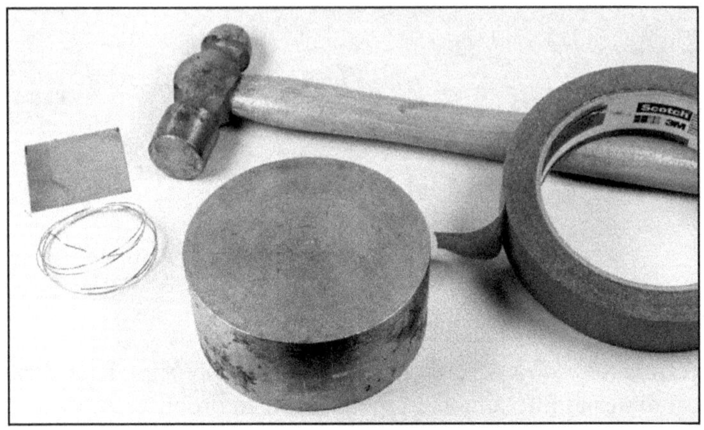

Tools and Supplies for a Wire Nest Texture

Applying the texture to a sheet is straightforward:

- Cut a length of wire - around 18 inches
- Ball-up most of it into a nest about an inch in diameter.
- Leave a short pigtail for holding the wire.
- Tape the sheet to be textured onto an anvil or bench block.
- Position the wire over your sheet.
- Hammer the nest while moving it around and changing its angle.

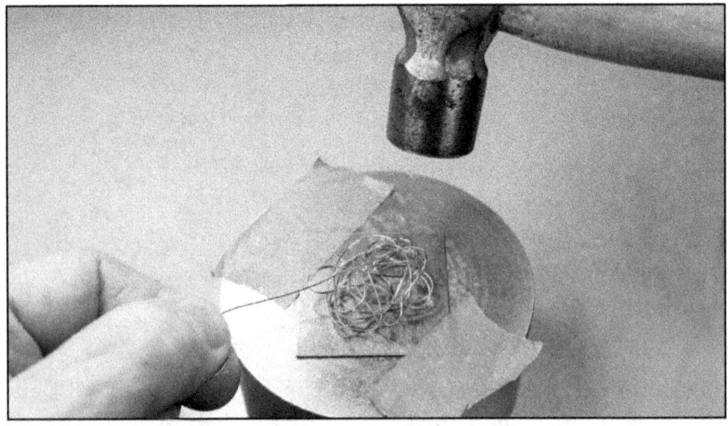

Applying a Wire Nest Texture

Texture 04 - Hammered Sandpaper

An evenly frosted, fine grain texture can be produced with a piece of coarse sandpaper using the same approach as with the wire nest. I've found a range of #40-#60 grit gives a particularly nice look.

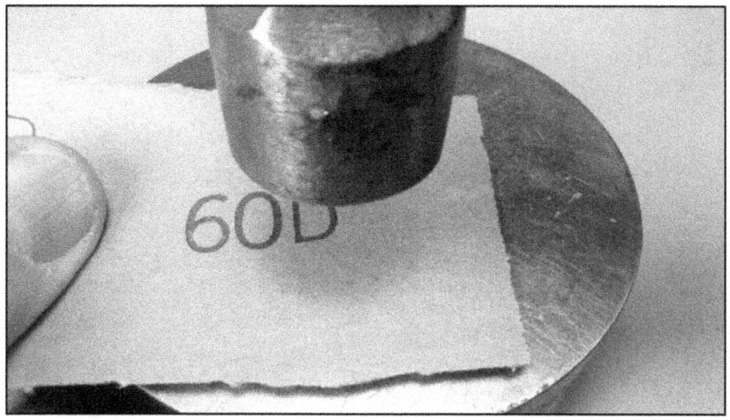

Applying a Sandpaper Texture

To produce these snowflake earrings in quantity, I made a mold and cast copies of the model that had been sawed from 16ga sheet. Unfortunately, the smooth, mirror finish of the castings required a lot more work than anticipated. #60 grit sandpaper frosted the surface without deforming them.

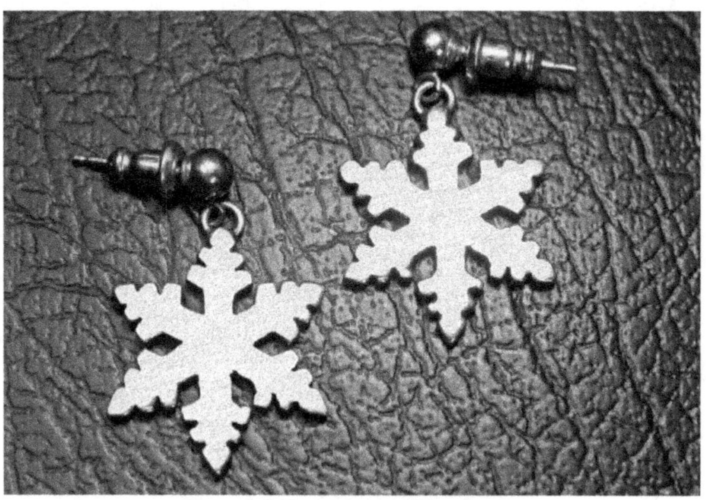

Frosted Texture on Earrings

CHAPTER 4

PUNCHES & STAMPS

Several different bold textures can be created using different sizes of stamps alone or in combination. Some of these stamps are available commercially. Others are created by making simple modifications to common tools that can be found at yard sales.

Texture 05 - Small Symbol Stamps

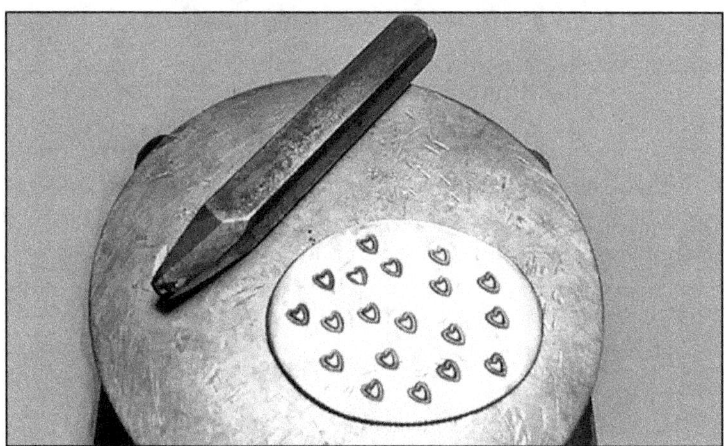

Design Stamp as a Texture Pattern

Design stamps are readily available from most jewelry tools suppliers. A small one can be used to quickly cover an area with multiple impressions. Symbol stamps like an asterisk * work well, and others like hearts or shamrocks celebrate special holidays. All that's needed is a utility hammer and a bench block or anvil. Different looks can be achieved by stamping the impressions in various patterns and/or alignments.

Texture 06 - Circular Stamps

This texture is a random, overlapping pattern of different sized circles applied with an inexpensive stamping tool. The tool is called a nail-set. They can be purchased online or at a hardware or building supplies dealer. You can also find them at flea markets.

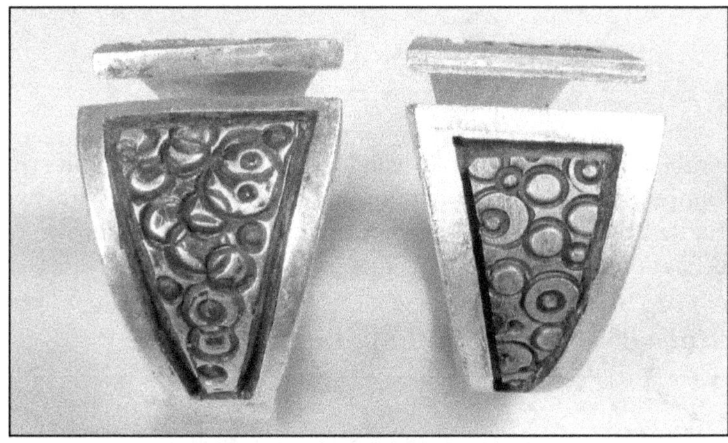

Example Ring Shanks with Bold Circle Textures

Nail-sets are used by carpenters to drive the head of a finishing nail down below the surface of the wood and are sold in a package of four or five different sizes. They're made from good quality steel and are designed to hold up well to a lot of pounding.

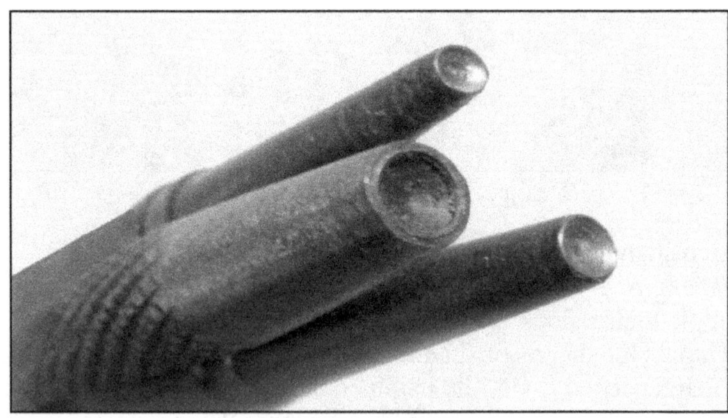

Tip of Nail-Set Tools

The working end of the tool has a rounded cavity to prevent it from slipping off the head of a nail. When the nail-set is hammered onto a sheet of metal, it's this rim that forms the circular impression. It makes a neat stamp for about $2 a piece.

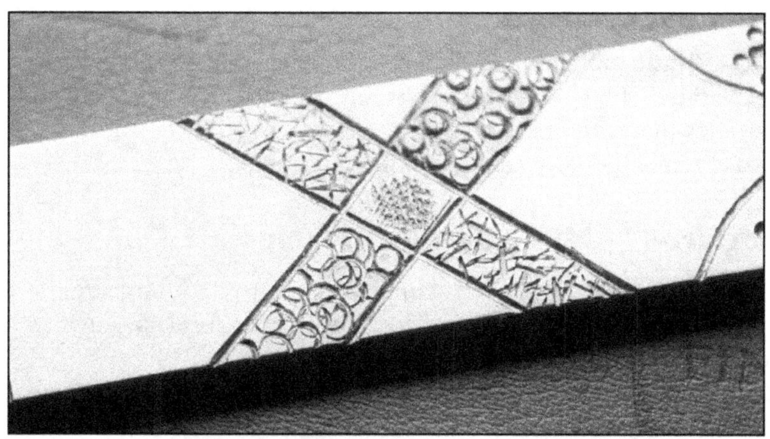

Some nail-sets purchased at yard sales or flea markets may show wear or damage on the rim of the rounded cavity, and those defects will show in any texture you create.

Any defect in the tip can be repaired rather easily with a diamond ball bur in the Foredom. It re-shapes the spherical cavity by cutting it deeper. Choose a bur that is the same or just a little larger in diameter than the old cavity. Check while cutting to be sure the outer rim has a uniform width all the way around. It's this rim that creates the circular impression on your jewelry piece.

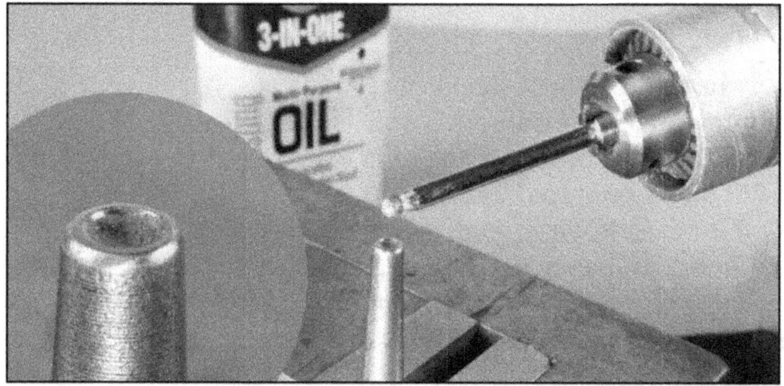

Note that diamond tools are the choice here because nail-sets are made from steel that has been hardened, somewhat like drill bits and files. A regular ball bur will not cut into it. But diamond bits have a hardness of 10 and can easily cut steels in the range of 5-1/2 to 6.

TIP - A little lubricating oil helps a lot when cutting into steel. It keeps the tool bit cooler so it lasts longer, and it flushes away small particles that tend to clog the cutting edges. And when cutting, please remember to wear your safety glasses.

Texture 07 - Mini Flat-Liner Stamps

Flat-liners are chisel shaped stamps that are used to form straight lines on a workpiece. They are commonly used for detailing an edge or creating a border.

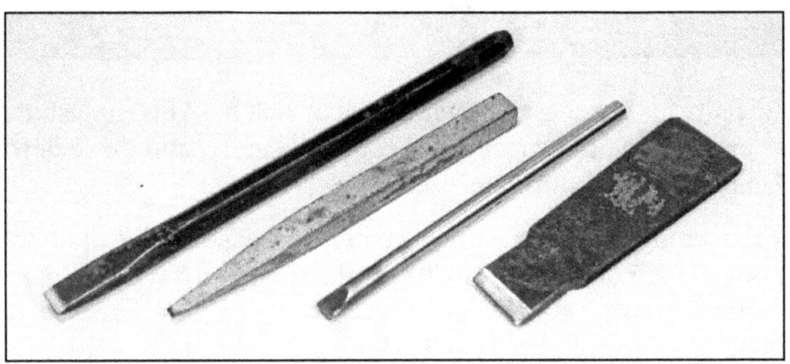

They come in a variety of widths to produce lines of different lengths from a quarter of an inch (12mm) up to one or two inches (25-50mm).

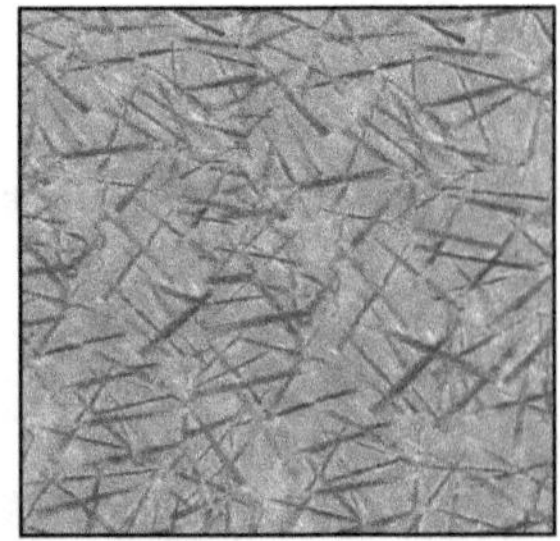

A very narrow flat-liner stamp can produce one of my favorite textures. It's smaller in every way. In the picture to the right, each straight line is produced by what I call a mini flat-liner. Its width is less than 1/8 inch (3mm). There are no commercial sources for them that I know of, but luckily they're rather easy to make. My preference is to modify one of the nail-set tools mentioned earlier for circle textures.

Nail-sets make great specialty tools for a number of reasons:

- Readily available and inexpensive.
- Good quality steel and convenient size.
- Changes only have to be made at the tip.
- Tapered shape allows good visibility of tip.
- Knurled surface gives a comfortable grip.

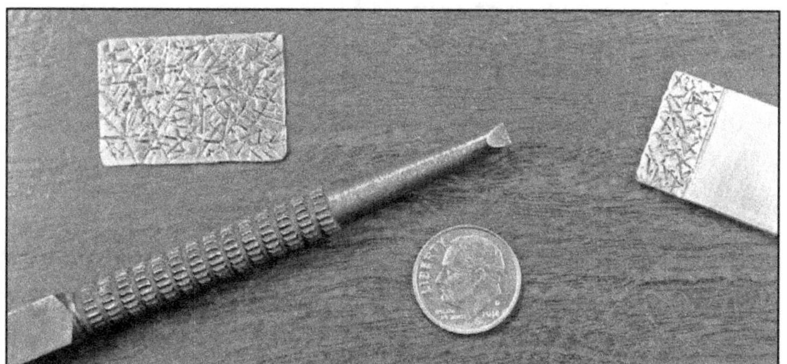

Modified Nail-Set with a Chisel Shaped Tip

The only modifications to be made on a nail-set are to shape the tip into a chisel edge. That is an easy task with most metals, but the hardened tool steel in nail-sets is more difficult and is best done with a sanding disc or fine grit grinding wheel in the Foredom or Dremel. See Appendix C for other options.

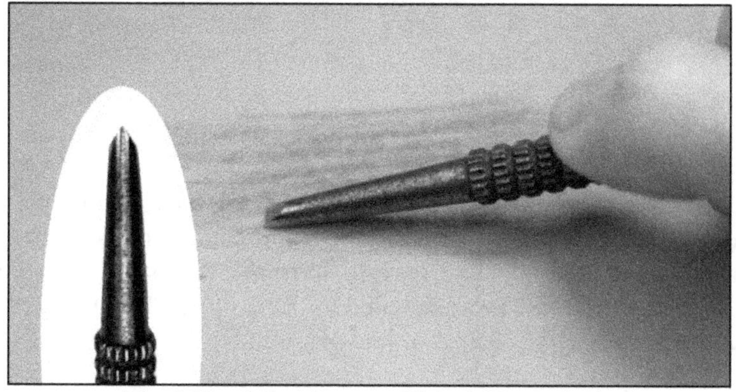

Final Hand Sanding on Chisel Shaped Tip

Final shaping is best done by hand using fine grit sandpaper (400-600) on a flat surface. Chisel angle shown is ~40 degrees.

TIP - Be careful when grinding or sanding hardened tools like a nail-set. Excess heating can soften the tip.

Texture 08 - Matting Tools

Matting tools are stamps often used by repoussé artists to add texture to surfaces or bottoms of recessed areas. These tools are commercially available and can be quite useful for texturing small areas of jewelry designs where a hammer cannot reach, where access is tight, or when the textured surface is close to a border or a soldered bezel or appliqué.

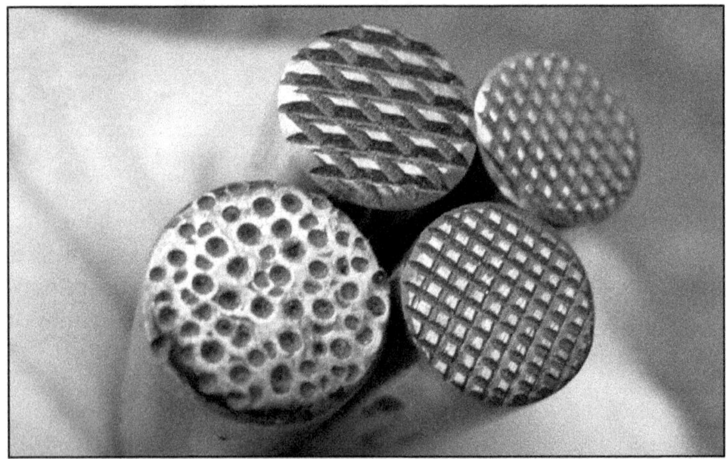

Matting Tools Made From 1/4" and 5/16" Rod

See Appendix A for several sources of matting tools.

Making one of your own is quite doable. It involves shaping the end of a steel punch and some simple heat treating operations to harden and toughen the tool for long term use. A good reference for those who would like more detailed information is "Making Design Stamps For Jewelry" See a brief description on Page 53.

CHAPTER 5

TEXTURING HAMMERS

Texture hammers are one of the easiest ways to add texture to flat sheet components for a jewelry project. The technique is fast, the tool is quite inexpensive, and the process requires little more than a bench block or anvil.

Ordinarily when a hammer is used in jewelry making, the head is polished so as to not leave any marks on the workpiece. Texturing hammers, on the other hand, are quite the opposite. They feature a carved face that is intended to leave a pattern on the material with each hammer swing.

Several are available commercially from various jewelry supplies companies. See Appendix B for sources. The hammers can also be made rather quickly from an old utility hammer from your tool box. Here are two example types that are easy to make yourself.

Texture 09 - Distressed Face Hammer

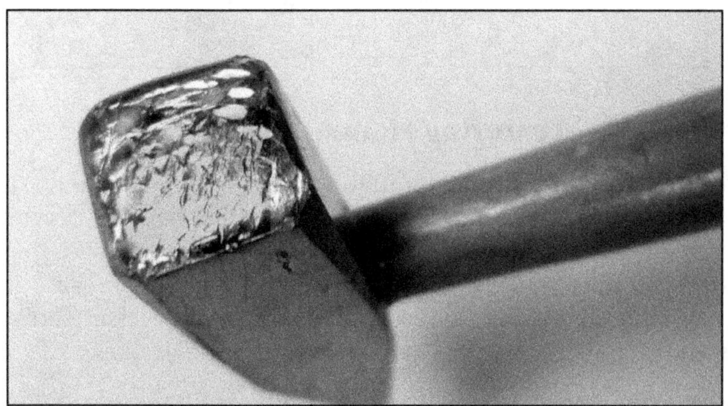

Distressed Pattern Texturing Hammer

Distressed may be another way of saying mistreated. In fact "Brutalized" is probably a more appropriate term for this hammer. The face was beaten against the corners of my anvil, then used to break up some ugly hard quartz, and finally had a couple divots cut into it with diamond bur bits.

This type of hammer is easy to create and is just as easy and efficient to use. I like them for applying a simple texture to hold a patina and minimize reflections or for a surface finish on the back side of a bracelet to hide the scratches that build up with long-term daily wear.

A second option for distressing a hammer is to carve its face with an assortment of different shaped diamond burs. Diamond is 10 on the Mohs Hardness scale, so it will easily cut into any variety of steel, which is in the range of 4.5 to 6.5 on the same scale. It's fun to experiment with your own designs.

Here's one example a carved hammer and the texture it produces:

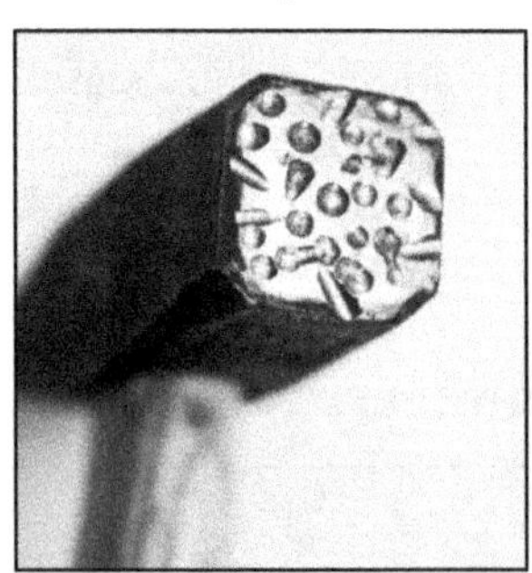

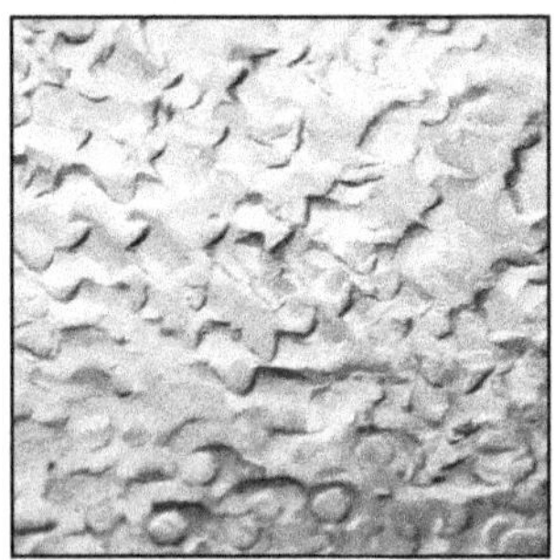

Texture 10 - Texturing Hammer

Even though I have a rolling mill to texture sheets of metal for my projects, I often prefer the simplicity of a texture hammer because it is so quick and easy to use. These hammers are made with designs cut or etched into their face specifically to impress a texture onto sheet stock. Typical patterns include checkerboards, repeating geometric designs, and various random designs.

These hammers are available commercially, but I was not too impressed after trying several of the lower-cost units for use in my adult-ed classes. The patterns seem to be too coarse, and the heads too large. The combination made it fairly difficult for me to get deep impressions on raw sheet metal. Higher priced hammers perhaps do not have that problem.

That prompted me to start modifying some existing hammers for student use, and I found it remarkably easy. Aside from a hammer, all that's needed is a a Foredom or Dremel motor-tool and a few separating discs from a jewelry supply company.

Separating discs come in a couple different thicknesses. The thinner ones are around 0.021 – 0.024 inches thick and seem to work best for the small face hammers that I modified.

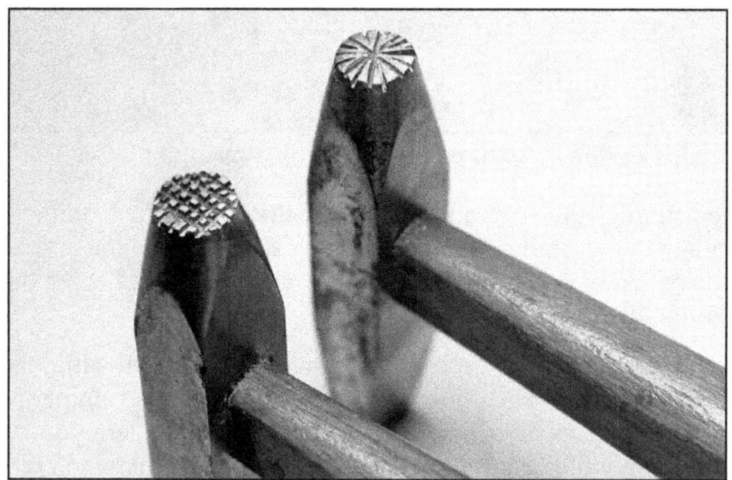

Checkerboard and Radial Pattern Texturing Hammers

As a reference, the faces on the hammers shown above are about a half inch (13mm) in diameter and the heads weigh about 3 ounces (85g). Notice that the cuts do not have to be very deep. These are probably less than one millimeter.

The checkerboard and radial patterns are easy to cut and produce a very pleasing texture. Diamond shaped patterns are another alternative.

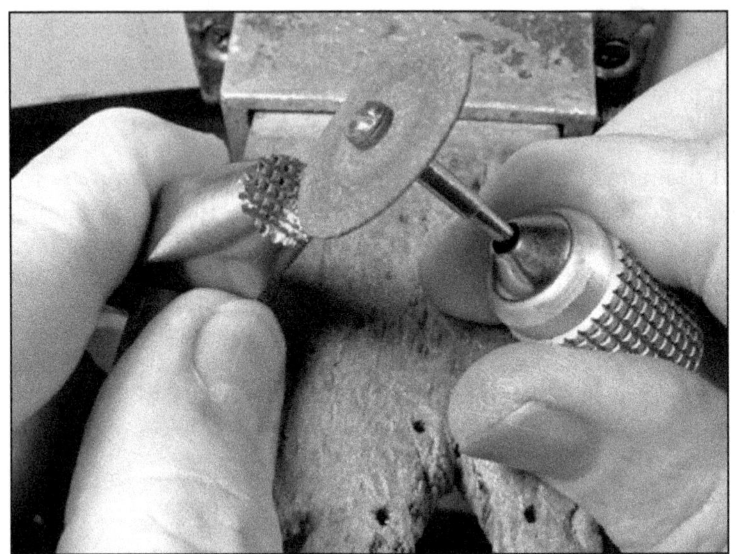
Carving a Texture Hammer With Separating Discs

When cutting with separating discs, be sure to hold the hammer and separating disc steady as you carve. Any wiggle while the disc is in the cut is likely to break the disc. In the picture above, I brace both hands on the bench pin.

Use a light pressure on each cut, and increase the depth with additional passes. When finished cutting, clean up the hammer face with fine sandpaper. And if you don't like the first pattern you create, simply file or grind it off and try cutting another one.

NOTE – A few cautions when using separating discs:

1. It's best to use a 1/8 inch diameter steel screw mandrel for the disc as thinner shafts may bend under the side pressures.
2. Use only straight line cuts. Trying to cut a curve will usually break the disc.
3. Please wear safety glasses. The debris coming off the disc is small particles of steel. It's best to hold the handpiece so that debris from the disc is thrown off to the side rather than directed straight at you.

CHAPTER 6

ROTARY BRUSHES

One of the easiest textures to apply is a fine satin finish done with a brass or steel brush. The coarseness of the texture can be varied by choosing the diameter of the wires and the material the wires are made from.

Thicker brush wires will produce a coarser satin texture, and steel wire will produce a coarser one than brass. So the coarsest finish will be obtained with thick steel wires, and the most subtle finish with thin brass wires.

NOTE - One caution is advised when using brass brushes on silver. It's best to keep the brush wet with soapy water to avoid any of the brassy color being transferred to the silver.

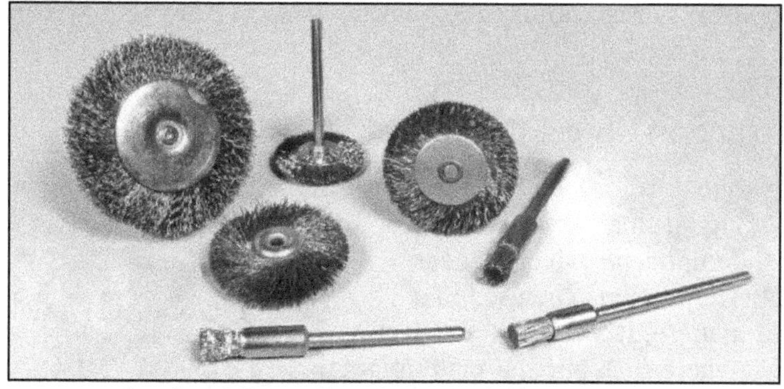

Steel and Brass Brushes Used for Texturing

Texture 11 - Brass Wheel Brush

Wheel type brushes have bristles that fan out radially. These work well on large areas of raw sheet to produce a light satin finish. Many artists prefer the fine satin finish to a mirrored polish.

Texture 12 - Steel Wheel Brush

Steel wires are more aggressive than brass. The satin finish produced is similar but more aggressive that with a brass wheel.

Texture 13 - Brass Cup Brush

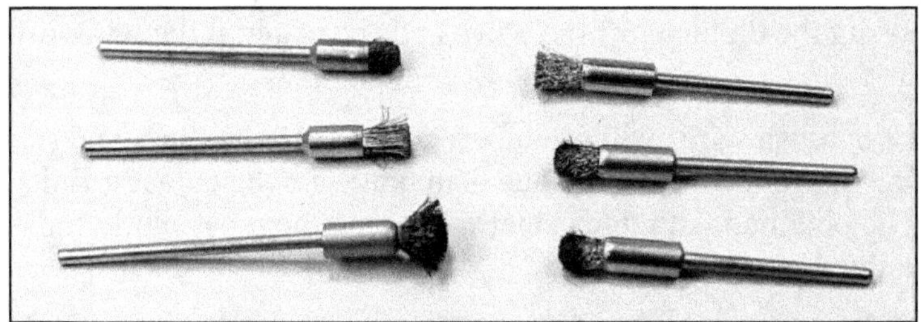

Brass and Steel Wire Cup Brushes

Cup style brushes have bristles in-line with the shaft of the tool. They're useful for cleaning the base plate between closely spaced components or the bottoms of pockets. Brass wires will leave only fine brush marks.

Texture 14 - Steel Cup Brush

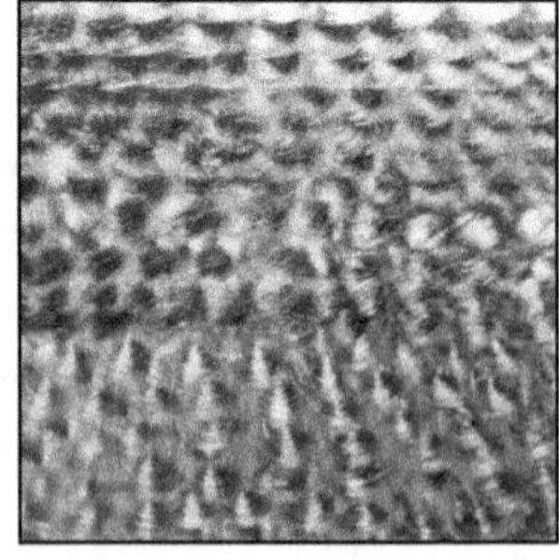

Cup style brushes are ideal for roughing up small areas between other components when space is tight. They can also be used in a linear pattern. It's called a jeweled finish where each circular pattern is overlapped by the adjacent patterns. Shown here, it was done with a 4mm diameter steel cup brush.

CHAPTER 7

ROTARY ABRASIVE BITS

Texture 15 - Cylindrical Abrasive Polisher

A simple Cratex or RTV rubber abrasive cylinder bit can be used to produce a texture of repetitive overlapping circular scored areas looking like a stack of coins that have fallen over in perfect arrangement. Jewelry folks call it a "jeweled" finish. I first encountered the texture in a machine shop where they called it a "machine" finish that helps to lubricate sliding parts of shop tools.

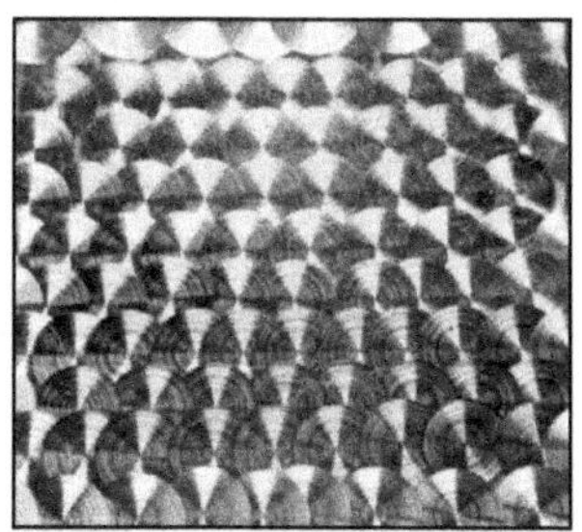

When experimenting with this texture, start with your coarsest cylinder bit. Note that the result will not be affected very much by the actual grit level.

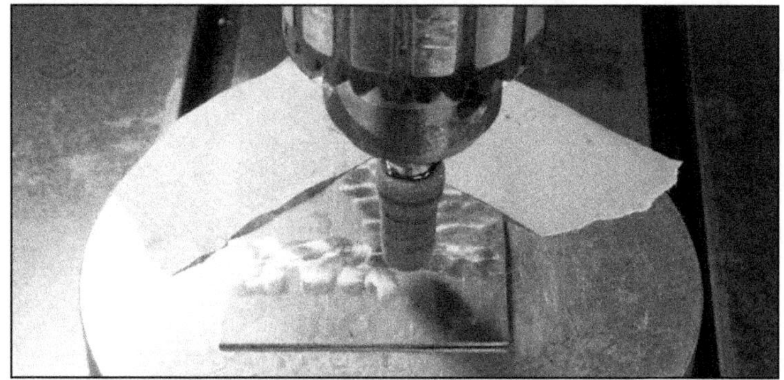

Abrasive Cylinder Bit in a Small Drill Press

Key to the technique is for each new circular impression to be located so that it overlaps adjacent impressions by the same amount.

Practice will be necessary to keep the line of swirls straight and evenly spaced. If you have some difficulty, try taping a straight-edge over the work to act as a guide.

While the texture can be applied with a Foredom or Dremel, it is sometimes easier to use a small drill press and move the workpiece around under the tool bit. Again, a straight-edge can be taped to the drill press table so the workpiece will slide along it generating a straight line of evenly spaced swirls.

Texture 16 - Coarse Bristle Discs

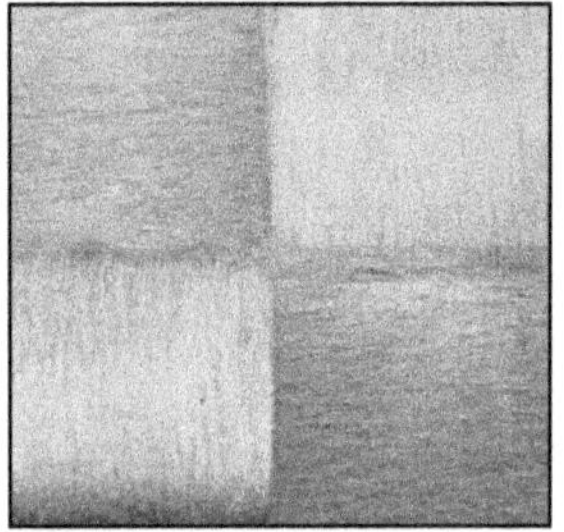

The bristle discs from 3-M are a very useful polishing tool. They contain an abrasive ceramic grit that's mixed into the plastic which forms the bristles. Grit level is indicated by disc color

The coarser units like the Green-50 grit or the Yellow-80 grit can be used to produce this useful surface finish that is good for hiding fingerprints.

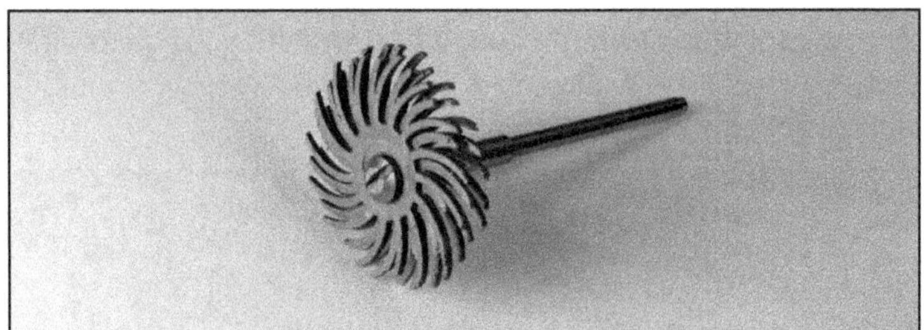

Coarse 50-Grit Bristle Disc

Finer bristle brushes like the Red -220 grit or the Blue -400 grit can be used to mute a texture that's looks too contrasty or to bring a scratched surface back to an even satin finish.

Note that when using bristle brushes, manufacturers recommend they work best when multiple discs are stacked on the same mandrel, usually 4-6 of them.

Texture 17 – Dental Sanding Discs

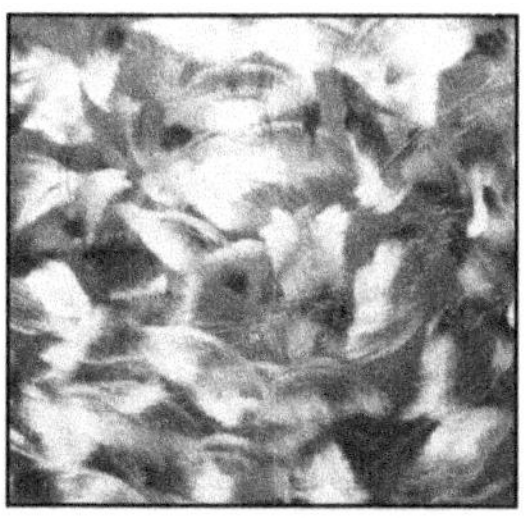

After first polishing the surface to be textured, the "slashed" pattern is applied with a small sanding disc by repetitively touching just the edge of the disc to the piece at a variety of different angles. This is a quick texture that works well for areas like the bottoms of cuff bracelets.

Normal jewelry size sanding discs (22mm) can certainly be used, but a more detailed jewelry-size pattern can be created with smaller discs.

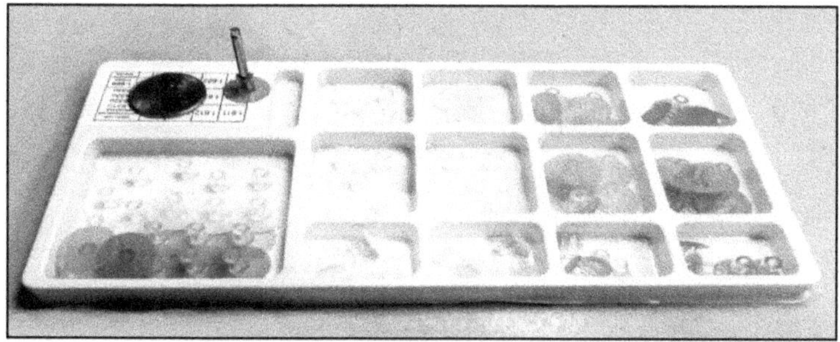

12mm Dental Sanding Disc Set

This set from the dental industry has a selection of discs that are only 12mm in diameter, and many have a flat face with no center screw that might scratch the workpiece. See the source list for supplies in Appendix A for more details.

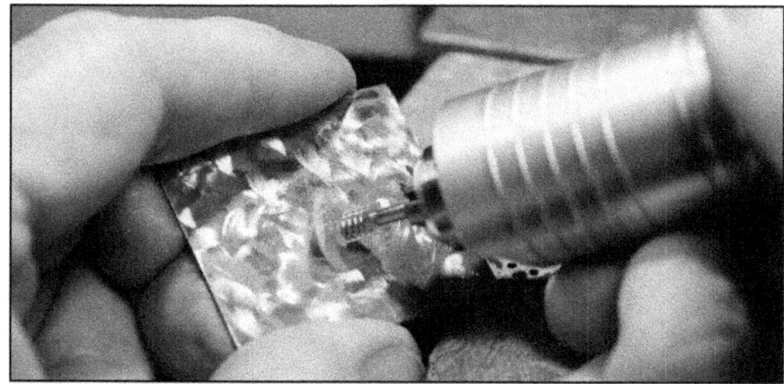

Applying a "Slashed" Pattern Texture

CHAPTER 8

HAMMER HANDPIECES

A hammer handpiece on a Foredom® converts the rotary motion of the motor into a woodpecker motion at the tip of the handpiece. Strength of the hammer blows is adjusted via a small ring near the center. With a flat anvil point (#2 below) screwed into the working end of the tool, stone setting is the typical use of these handpieces.

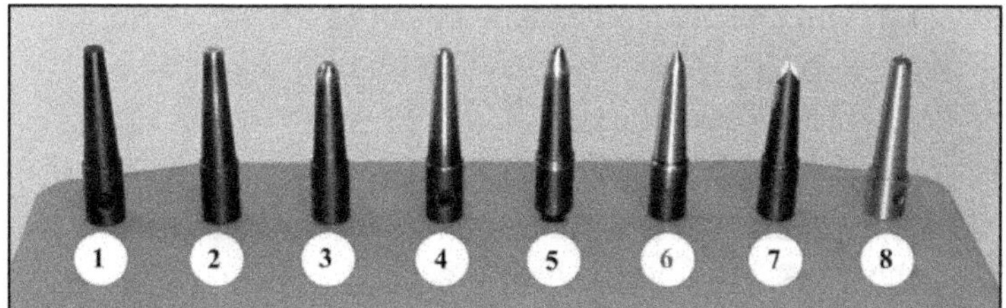

Variety of Different Anvil Point for Hammer Handpiece

It's also possible to purchase blank anvil points (#1) and customize the tips for special tasks like texturing. Each hammer blow then creates an indentation on the surface of the jewelry item, and repeated indentations form a texture.

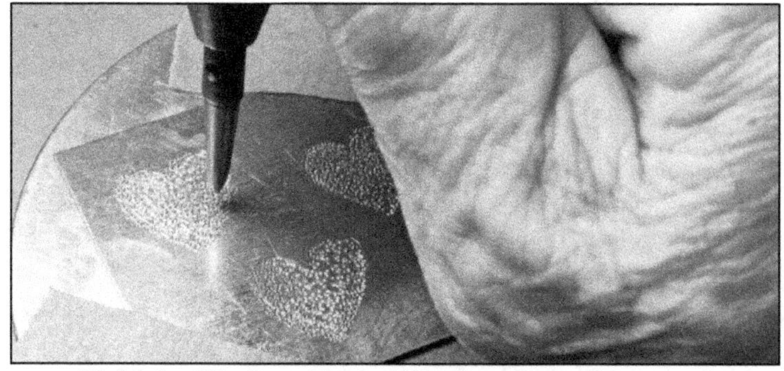

Hold the Tip Just Clear of Surface Being Textured

Handpieces are very useful in this mode. I find I do as much texturing as I do stone setting. Textures can be added exactly where you need them and right up to a specific boundary.

NOTE - Handpieces do have limitations with how much force they can deliver. Larger anvil geometries will not produce as much depth in a texture as will smaller and sharper anvil geometries.

To get the best texturing:

- Place the workpiece on a bench block or plate of steel.
- When holding the handpiece, position the anvil point slightly above the metal surface to get the most powerful hits.
- Move the anvil point in small circles as you 'paint' the surface with texture. It looks best when the indentations are random and are in the same density across the entire surface. Avoid moving in a straight line as those indentations tend to catch the eye.
- Avoid running the flexshaft motor at too high a speed. This can generate excessive heat and increase the wear on both the flex-shaft and the handpiece.
- Be careful not to bend the flexshaft sheath or the handpiece spring more than specified in the operating manual.

Texture 18 - Stipple Anvil Point

If you try making only one of these anvil points, the sharp pointed stipple (Anvil Point #6) is the one I'd suggest. It's shaped like a narrow-angle, sharp center punch and produces a beautiful texture that is easily controllable. This heart was sketched on a copper sheet and then "painted" with a stippled texture to add emphasis.

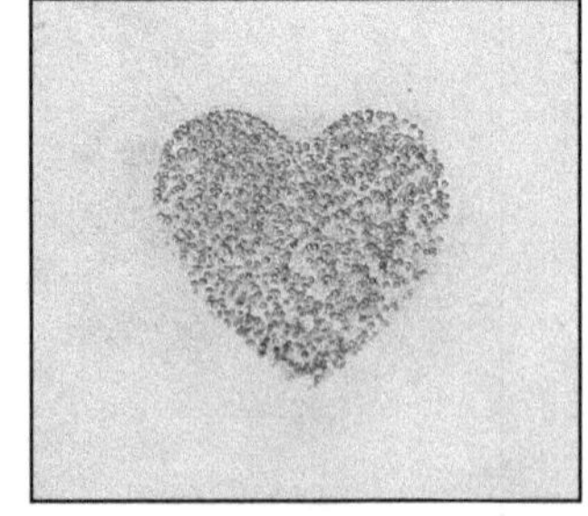

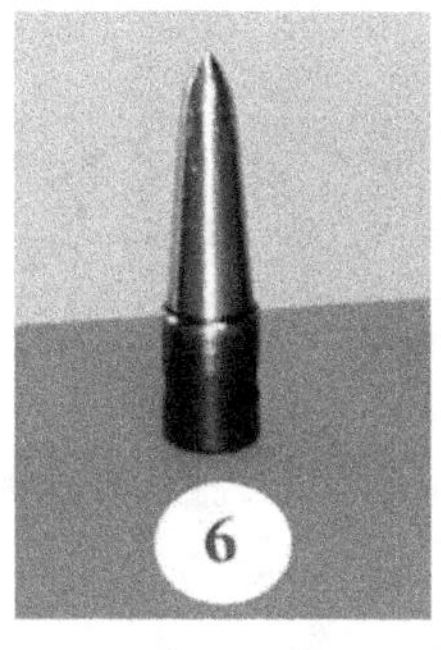

Making one of the tips from a blank anvil point (#1) goes very quickly. Since the blanks are made from hardened steel, you will not be able to shape them with a file. The steel blank is too hard.

Rough shaping can be done with a sandpaper disc or a diamond disc in the Foredom. It can also be done by hand with grindstone or a diamond file.

To finish the conical point, place it in the Foredom handpiece and spin the tip on a sheet of sandpaper that is taped to a flat surface. Finally, I give it a quick polish on the buffer with Tripoli or Zam. See Appendix C for more options on working with steel.

Texture 19 - Round Anvil Point

Anvil Points #3, #4 and #5 are shaped with small, medium and large rounded tips for producing mini versions of the hammered textures done with ball peen hammers.

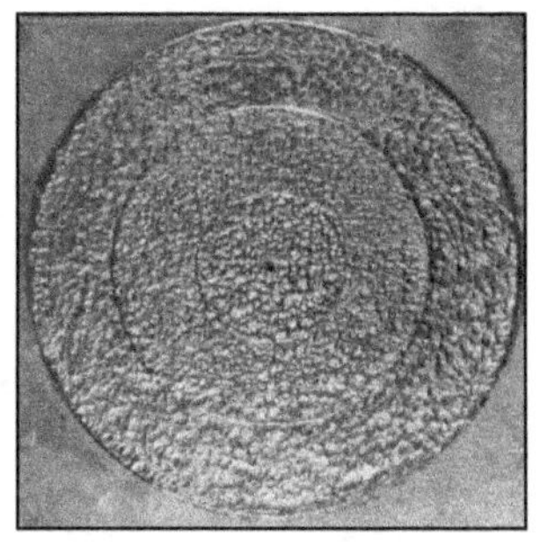

The innermost circle was done with the smallest tip (#3) - about 1.5mm in diameter.

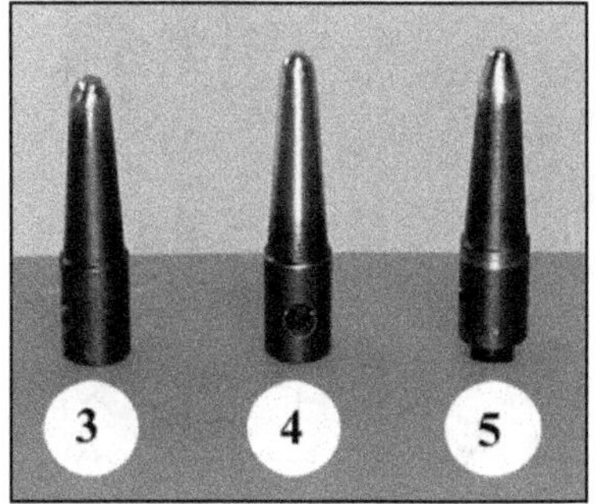

The middle band was done with the medium tip (#4) - 2mm in diameter.

The outermost circular band was done with the largest anvil tip (#5) - about 3mm in diameter.

Texture 20 - Chisel Anvil Point

Anvil point #7 is shaped as a narrow chisel, about 3mm in width. The chisel angle must be shaped quite sharply to get a reasonable depth of the impressions. Hammer handpieces are not able to generate the force needed by larger chisel points.

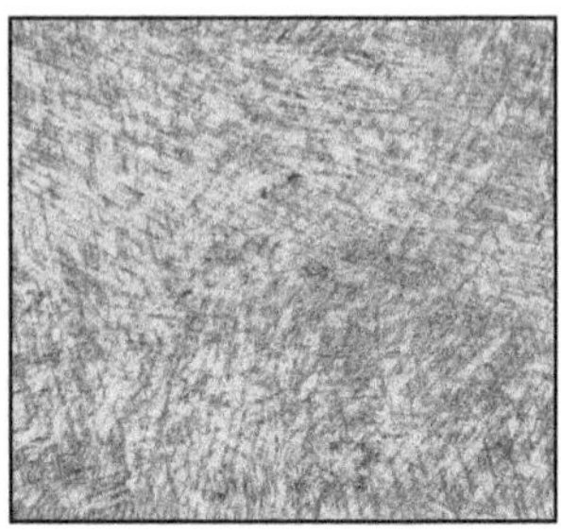

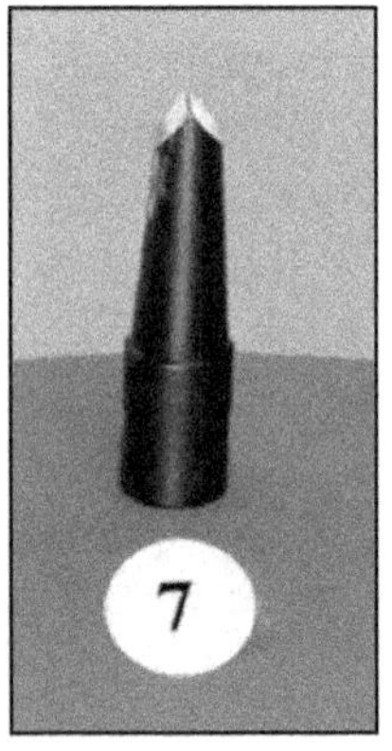

An anvil blank is quite small and difficult to hold while modifying its tip into a chisel shape. I grip the blank in a bur holder or pin vise, and that helps to orient it rather easily. Rough shaping is done first with a grinder or 300 grit sandpaper taped onto a flat surface.
Final shaping is done by hand on 600 grit sandpaper. You may want to use a loupe in checking progress of the shaping.

Notice the shallow angle of the pin vise from the horizontal. I try to keep it at about 20-degrees or less. The resulting chisel point has an included angle of about 40-degrees.

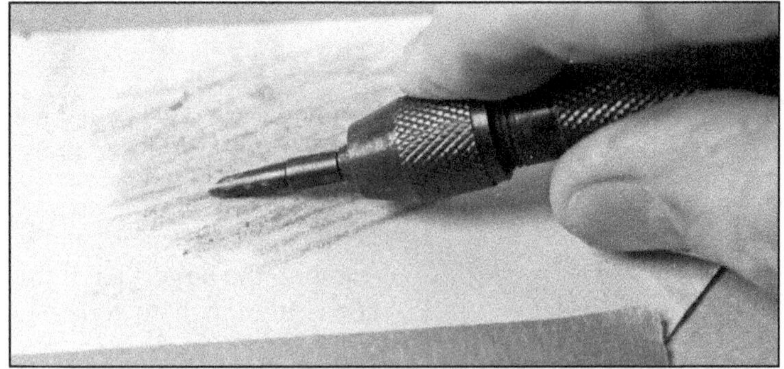

Creating a Chisel Point on an Anvil Blank

Texture 21 - Diamond Anvil Point

Anvil Point #8 is a little different in that has a small diamond set upside down at its tip. The point is also called a pavé tip, available from most large tools suppliers. Each indentation impresses the shape of the diamond culet into the workpiece creating a bright, reflective texture pattern.

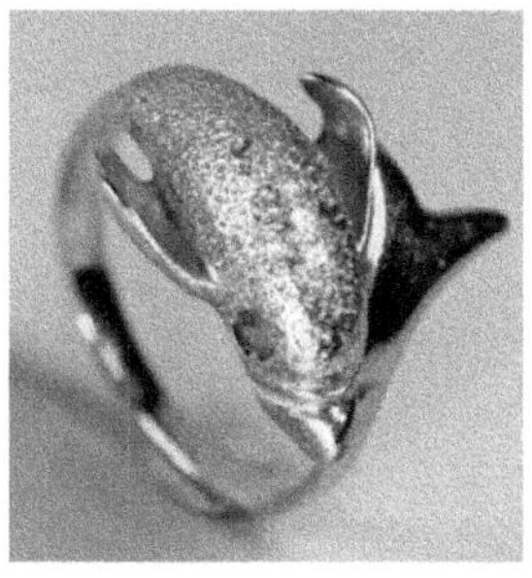

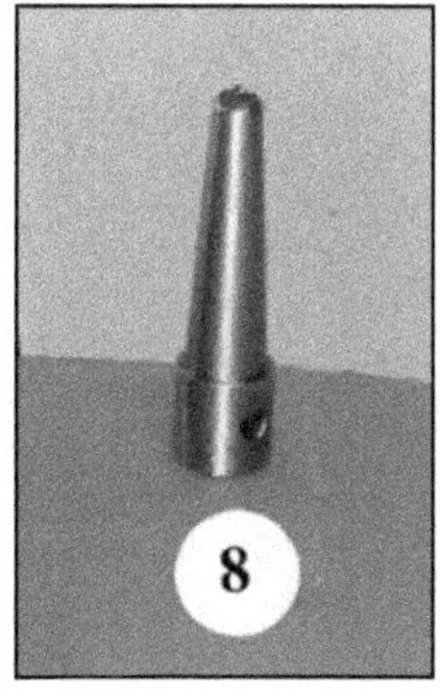

The texture is quick to apply. Keep the tip just above the surface and move it continuously in small circles to get an even density of indentations.

NOTE - A pavé texture is very fine and looks great, but is best used only on gold. On silver, the very fine indentations will eventually tarnish and cannot be re-polished.

Here's a better example of the texture on a 14ky gold ring and earring set obtained with the pavé tip. Texturing was done after all other work was finished and the surface had been buffed to a mirror finish.

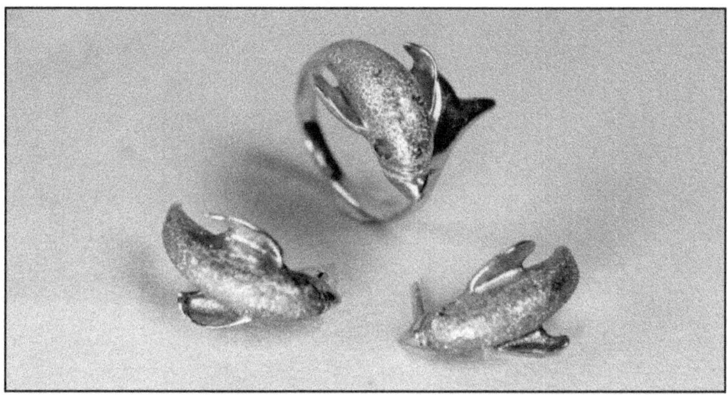

Diamond Textured Dolphin Ring and Earring Set in 14ky.

CHAPTER 9

MISCELLANEOUS TEXTURES

Lastly are a few of my favorites that are very simple but do not fall into one of the more common categories.

Texture 22 - Diamond Ball Bur

Another type of satin finish can be applied with a diamond ball bur. My preference is one about 6-8mm in diameter and 150 grit. Applying the finish can be done at any stage of fabrication.

Stroke the ball bur across the metal surface in a linear direction with a light, constant pressure. Repeat with closely overlapping linear strokes to cover.

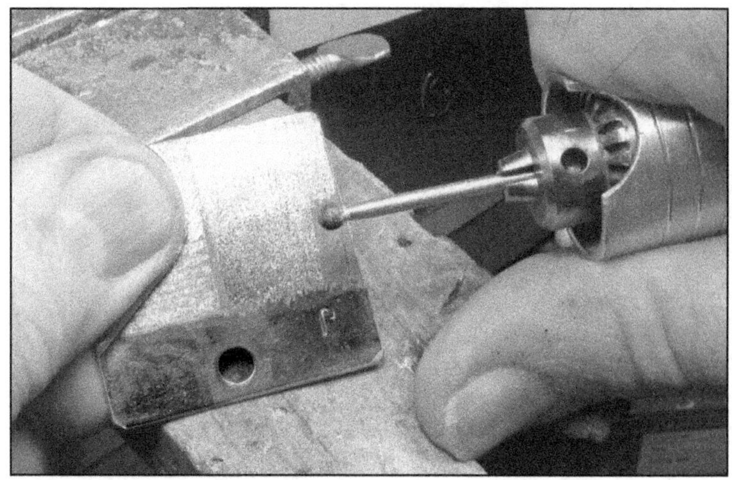

Applying a Diamond Ball Bur Texture

Texture 23 - Broken Drill

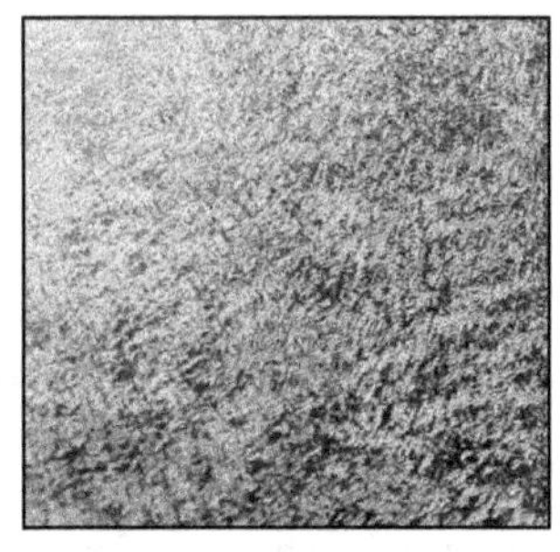

One very simple technique for adding a quick texture whenever needed is to use a broken drill bit. Yes, it is really that easy. Look for an old drill that's dull and worn out, preferably one that's about 2mm in diameter (#44 - #50)

To prepare the drill for texturing, clamp the tip in a vise or set of strong pliers, and break it off to expose fresh sharp edges. Be sure to wear safety glasses. Then place the drill in the Dremel or Foredom and try it out.

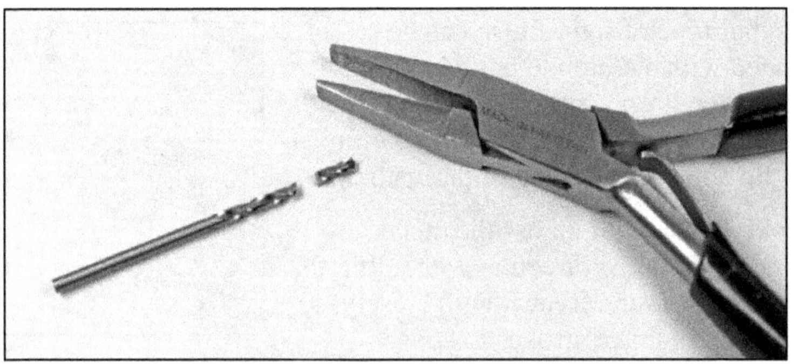

Broken Drill as a Texturing Tool

Texture 24 – Rotary Texture Wheel

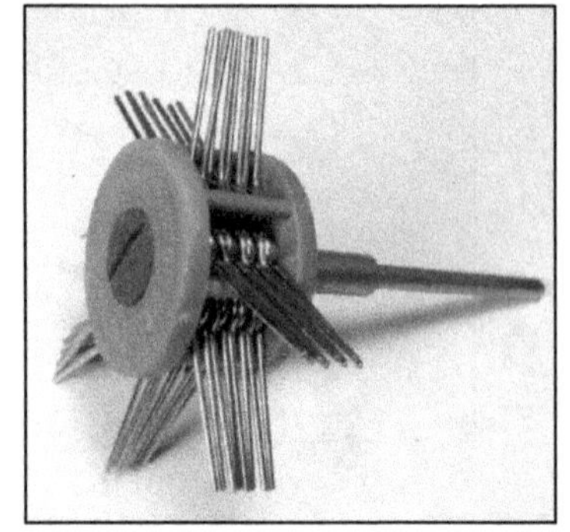

These texturing wheels are a little expensive but are definitely worthwhile if you like the even pattern they produce and make use of a fair amount of textured sheet in your work.

CAUTION is advised with this tool. You do not want to texture your fingers. Wear a full face shield, hold smaller pieces with pliers, and run the flexshaft motor at a slow speed.

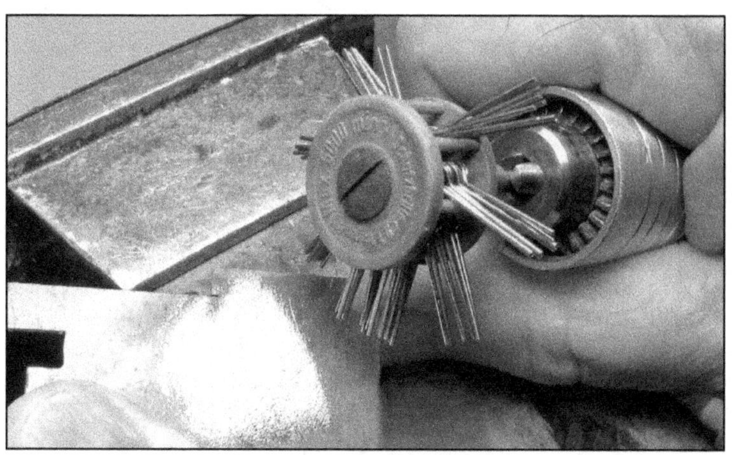

Rotary Texture Wheel

A FAVOR PLEASE

Reviews are a significant way for books to gain visibility. As an independent author, I hope you enjoyed

24 Easy Metal Textures

and I'd truly appreciate it if you could post a few words of review on Amazon

Amazon.com/dp/B0BPGPTBNH/

- Thank you

ABOUT THE AUTHOR

Brad Smith is a studio jeweler, lapidary, and jewelry instructor in Santa Monica, CA. He enjoys working with silver, gold, exotic woods, bone, fossil ivory, and meteorite.

As a long-time member of the Culver City Rock Club, Brad has taught lapidary skills, led field trips, organized gem and mineral shows, helped run their lapidary shop, and served in most of the club positions, including President. He is also a member of the Metal Arts Society of Southern California.

His teaching career started in the Los Angeles school system where he taught Advanced Jewelry in the Adult Education Department for eight years. Then in 2009, he was invited to design and build a new jewelry facility at the Santa Monica Adult Education Center where he taught beginning and advanced classes for nine years.

Brad also likes photography & scuba diving, develops websites, and moderates several jewelry making and rockhounding discussion groups on the Internet.

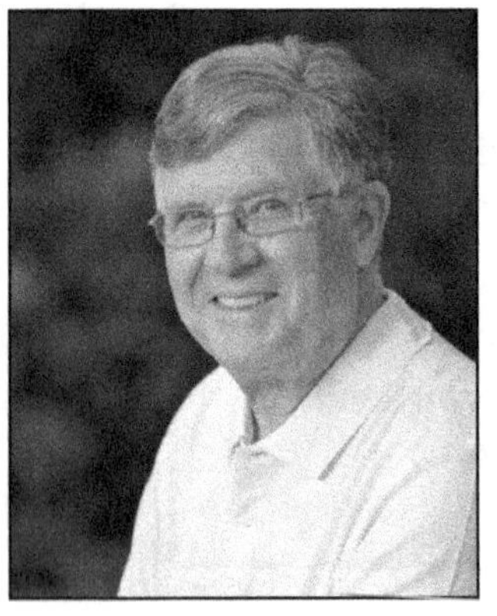

Contact the author at
BradSmith Jewelry@gmail.com

or see his website at

http://BradSmithJewelry.com/

APPENDIX - A

TEXTURING MATERIALS & SUPPLIES

Dental Sanding Discs

12mm Dental Sanding Disc Set
amazon.com/ dp/B08BCTP8LL/

Textured Sheet

Metalliferous - New York, NY
24ga Brass Pattern Sheet 2.5" wide by the foot
www.metalliferous.com/Brass-Patterned-Strip/products/2873/

Cool Tools - Jefferson, WI
Copper, Brass, Bronze, Fine Silver, Sterling, Argentium
www.cooltools.us/Textured-Metals-s/1797.htm

Halstead Bead - Prescott, AZ
Copper, Brass, Bronze, Fine Silver, Sterling, Argentium
www.halsteadbead.com/sheet-metal

FDJ Tool - Sanford, FL
Copper, Brass, Aluminum, Sterling
www.fdjtool.com/metals

Low Cost Hammers for Making a Texturing Tool

Beadsmith Ball Peen XTL-2150
amazon.com/gp/product/B00158BDM0/

Separating Discs

Rio Grande Supply - Albuquerque, NM
- - riogrande.com/ Part # 337298

APPENDIX - B

SOURCES FOR TEXTURING TOOLS

Hammer Handpiece Points

FDJ Tool - Sanford, FL
- - fdjtool.com/
Part # 431106 thru 431111

Rio Grande Supply - Albuquerque, NM
- - riogrande.com
Part # 117118

Santa Fe Jewelers Supply- Santa Fe, NM
- - sfjs.net
Part # 53.195

Liner Stamps

Chris Pruitt Stamps - Paguate, NM - Chris Pruitt
- - cpruitttools.com/

Ferro Valley Tool - Albuquerque, NM - Danny Wade
- - ferrovalleytools.com/

The House of Stamps - Gallup, NM
- - thehouseofstamps.com/

Matting Tools

Chris Pruitt Stamps - Paguate, NM - Chris Pruitt
- - cpruitttools.com/

FDJ Tool - Sanford, FL
- - fdjtool.com/
    Part # PN7100 thru PN7124

Charles Lewton Brain -. Calgary, Canada
- - lewtonbrain@gmail.com

Texturing Brushes

Otto Frei Jewelry Supply – Oakland, CA
- - OttoFrei.com/
    Part #111.490 thru 111.499

Rio Grande Supply - Albuquerque, NM
- - riogrande.com/
    Part # 338250, 338217, 338218, 338219

Texturing Hammers

Otto Frei Jewelry Supply – Oakland, CA
- - OttoFrei.com/
    Part # 137.135KIT, 137.135MAIN, 137.216

Santa Fe Jewelers Supply- Santa Fe, NM
- - sfjs.net/
    Part # 380681, 380682 and 380683

APPENDIX - C

WORKING WITH STEEL

As metalsmiths, we are comfortable working with different metals like copper, silver, and perhaps gold. We know a little about alloys - the mixtures of metals like brass, bronze, and Sterling. And we sometimes use different colors of metal like Shibuichi or gold. We're familiar with metalworking processes for cutting, shaping, forging, burring, drilling, sanding, and polishing. And we are aware of the characteristics of metals like how they get harder as we hammer or bend them and softer when we anneal them. The more we know about the metals we work with, the more capable and comfortable we are at the jewelry bench.

But at the same time I watch new metalworkers becoming familiar with our jewelry metals, I notice their reluctance to make any changes to their steel tools. Maybe they feel it takes special machines to cut, shape, drill, sand, or polish it. But whatever the reason is, I think it's unfortunate because:

- Our tools often need maintenance and care.
- Some can be modified to do their job faster or better.
- Old tools can be re-purposed for custom tasks.
- Better tools can encourage better quality work.

I've found it very worthwhile to always be open to modifying the tools and procedures I'm using. And I've cut enough steel to know that common hand tools are all that's needed to handle most of the tool maintenance and modification I want to do.

This appendix is included to help those who wish to know more about keeping their tools in good shape or modifying them a bit to get improved performance.

Dressing New Tools

New tools as purchased are not always in the optimum condition to be used right out of the box. Sometimes they have to be modified a bit before they're ready for your bench work. I've had pliers with such sharp edges that they leave a mark on the workpiece. I get burnishers with tips that will cut you if the tool slips a bit. And I've had hammer faces with sharp edges that left crescent-shaped depressions whenever the angle of the hit wasn't perfect.

Fixing these minor problems with a new steel tool is quite easy. I call it "dressing" the tool - getting it ready to work for you. Usually all it takes is a file, some sandpaper, and a polish on your buffer.

Dressing a tool starts with a careful inspection of the working end of the tool, the part of the tool that will contact your workpiece. The surfaces need to be smooth with no bumps, grooves or scratches that could transfer onto your metal. Look for any sharp edges. Sand any area that may be a problem. Then give the tool faces a good polish on the buffer with an aggressive compound like Tripoli or Zam.

This dressing process is important in that it saves you time. I figure that any nick or scratch that my tools put on a workpiece is going to cost me a extra 10 or 20 minutes to correct.

Maintaining Older Tools

Older steel tools will rarely need any major work. Maintenance or rejuvenation generally involves a polishing or a minor re-shaping of the working end - as on a hammer, a center punch, or a chisel. Usually the only supplies needed are sandpaper or some sanding sticks.

I prefer starting with fine sandpaper, around 400 grit. It does the least damage to the tool surface and requires only a polish to finish up afterwards. Fine sandpaper will at least clean the surface and let you see any irregularities.

Any large flats, bumps or scratches can then be removed with coarse sandpaper either by hand or with a sanding disc in the Foredom. Then it's back to the fine sandpaper for smoothing out the scratches left by the coarse sandpaper. Finally, my preference is to give the tool a good polish on the buffer with a compound like Tripoli or Zam.

Reshaping a Tool

If the shape of a hammer or other tool needs to be modified a lot, the best hand tool to use is a file. They are quite versatile and come in three different levels of coarseness.

After filing the new tool shape, remove file marks with coarse sandpaper like 150 grit and follow the finishing sequence mentioned earlier with 400 grit sandpaper and a polish on the buffer.

NOTE - Working on steel is hard work for a file. It's best to not use your expensive jewelry files on steel. Inexpensive flat mill files can be purchased for under $10 from Amazon or from your local hardware store or builders supply outlet.

Quality of Steels

When trying to re-shape the face of some tools, you may find a file will not bite into the steel and kind of slide across it. This indicates the tool is made from better quality steel than used for common items like brackets, nails, bolts and nuts.

Good quality steels can be heat treated to make them harder and more durable than common steels. This translates into better performance. Tools stay sharper, and the working ends don't deform as much during long-term use.

The fact that some steel tools are harder than others allows a file to re-shape the end of a steel screwdriver, a drill bit to pierce a steel plate, and a saw blade to cut through a steel bolt. The tool being used is harder than the piece being cut. In fact, a tool always has to be harder for it to be able to cut into or even scratch a workpiece.

Common steels and quality steels look alike, but a file will help you detect which is which. Files are always made of hardened tool steel. They will cut any material that is softer, and they will tend to skate across the surface of any material that is harder. So they're a good way to test for hardness.

If the tool you want to modify turns out to be a good quality steel, you will need to choose another material that has a higher hardness to cut and shape it, so let's look at the hardness scale of alternatives.

The Hardness Scale

Hardness is worth knowing about, especially if you need to cut into and re-shape something like a punch or nail-set that is hardened steel. The tool bit doing the cutting must always be harder than the piece being modified. One of the ways to describe the hardness of different materials is the "Mohs" scale. The softest material is Talc chalk ranking as a 1, and the hardest is Diamond ranking as a 10.

Here are some common materials that metalsmiths work with and where each places on the hardness scale:

Talc chalk 1.0

Silver 2.8

Brass 3.0

Common Steel 4.5

Hardened Steel 6.5

Silicon Carbide Abrasive 9.5

Diamond 10

If the tool you are working on is made from good quality, hardened steel, you'll need to use something harder than a file to shape it. The best options are silicon abrasive sandpaper, a diamond file, or diamond sandpaper. Then follow the earlier finishing sequence of finer sanding and buffer polishing.

Foredom and Dremel

While hand tools can be used to cut, smooth and sand steel surfaces like the face of a hammer, removing larger amounts of material is more labor intensive. If that's the case, the best approach is to use some motorized equipment.

The first alternative I consider is the Foredom or Dremel tools common in the jewelry workshop. There is an enormous variety of bits available for these tools, particularly in the abrasive grit category that works well on steel.

For those who would like more detailed information on choosing the best bits to use, a good reference is "Accessories for the Foredom and Dremel" See a brief description of this book on Page 57.

For bits to re-shape steel tools with the Foredom or Dremel, look for grinding bits and sanding discs.

Grinding Bits

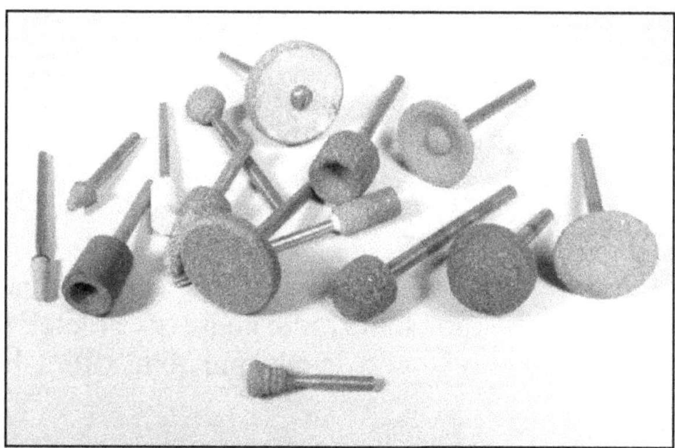

Grinding Bits in Various Shapes and Grit Levels

You have probably seen these in a kit of assorted rotary bits. They are a coarse abrasive (Hardness 9.5) and good for grinding hard metals like steel (Hardness 4.5 - 6.5). They're also useful when shaping some of your own metal tools or making new ones. They come in different shapes and coarseness levels. Choose the shape for the desired cut and the grit level for the speed of metal removal.

Sanding Bits

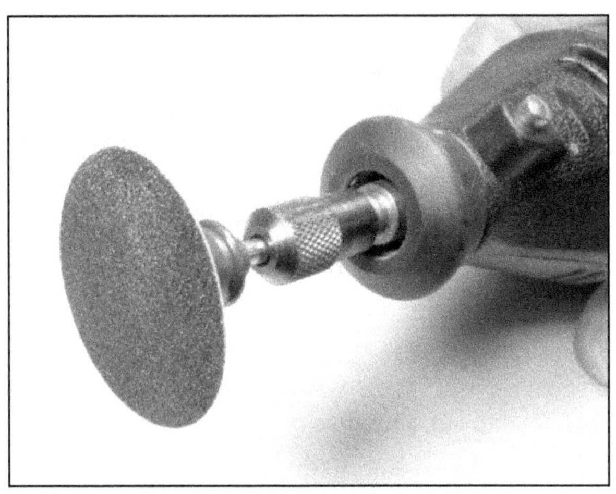

Dremel Sanding Discs in Varied Grit Levels

The Dremel® EZ Lock™ system offers large, flat sanding discs without any center screw head. Discs are a generous 1.50 inches in diameter and come in 60 grit, 120 grit, and 240 grit (Hardness 9.5). These make quick work of smoothing surfaces that have been roughly shaped with grinding bits.

Motorized Bench Tools

If you start to work a lot with steel and if you have the space, it's well worthwhile to look for some more aggressive motorized bench tools. I've found them to be very handy and quite affordable.

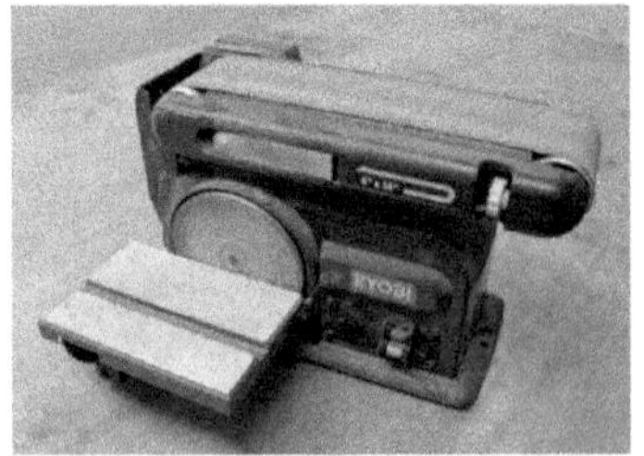

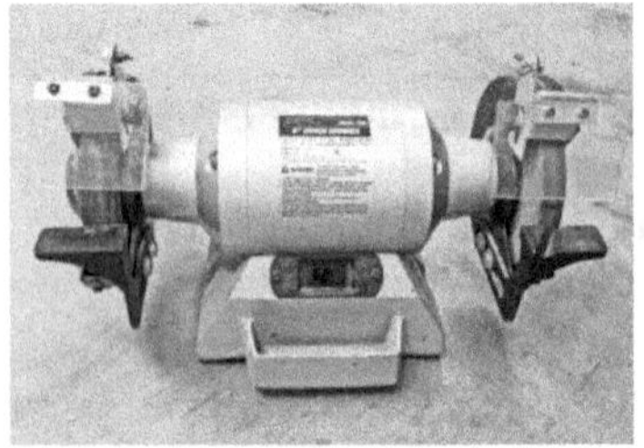

OTHER BOOKS BY THE AUTHOR

Making Design Stamps for Jewelry

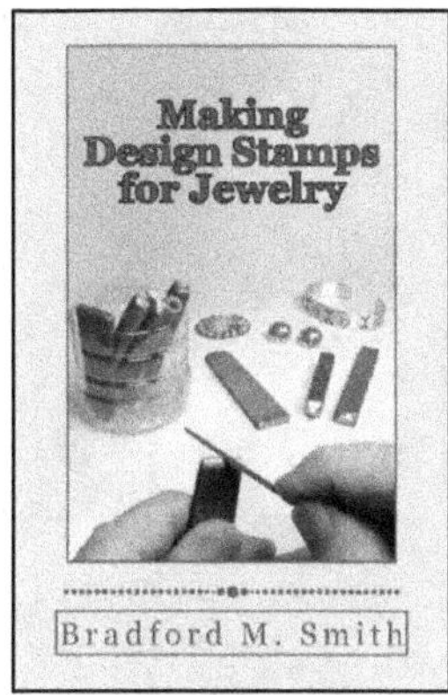

Learn how to create unique stamps and texturing tools to add visual interest to your work, for a special application, or to brand your pieces with a stamp that others cannot purchase. These customized tools embellish your jewelry designs and can be made with common jewelry tools and techniques. There are only a few differences in working with steel as compared to copper or silver.

The volume covers the step-by-step process of selecting best steels, carving the design, hardening the steel, and tempering it to ensure a long service life. It describes the tools to use, gives detailed examples for making several stamps, includes sources for tool steel, describes useful shop equipment, and has tips for saving time and achieving better quality.

amazon.com/dp/098828586X/

Editorial Review

"A must have book for the metalsmith"
- Danny Wade, Ferro Valley Tool, LLC and
creator of the Metal Stamp Addicts group on Facebook.

Amazon Reader Review

- This book is absolutely wonderful! If you are at all interested in the very least in making your own jewelry stamps, then you definitely need this book. At 68 pages, I was initially hesitant, but I was wrong; this book is jam-packed with a plethora of information, all of which is totally relevant, and revealing

Bench Tips for Jewelry Making

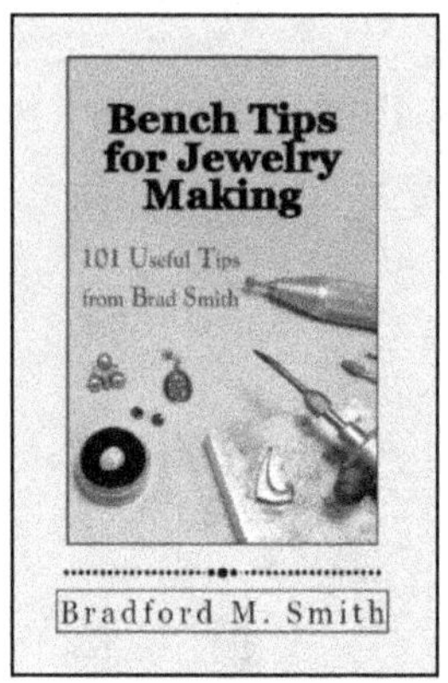

In every field, the top artisans have their favorite ways of solving common problems. Making a piece of fine jewelry is no exception. Accomplished jewelers have a variety of techniques, special tools and shortcuts that are proven to save time and improve quality.

This book is written as a resource for jewelers with skill levels from beginner through advanced. The bench tips come from Brad Smith's twenty years of experience in the jewelry industry, including over a decade teaching hundreds of students.

The tips include over twenty ways to save time when soldering and polishing, eight common hazards to avoid, many ways to cut costs, ten tips to improve stone setting skills, and the "must-have" tools for increasing productivity at the bench.

amazon.com/dp/0988285800/

Editorial Reviews

This small treasure covers a multitude of solutions to a myriad of issues facing the jewelry artisan…The easy to understand text and very good photographic black and white images makes this book quite self-explanatory…

- Razine Wenneker - Founder, The Society for Midwest Metalsmiths

This is a well written reference book by a very experienced studio jeweler and classroom instructor. The photographs and diagrams clearly point out the finer points of the various tips he demonstrates…

- Bruce Carlson - Florida Society of Goldsmiths Newsletter

Broom Casting For Creative Jewelry

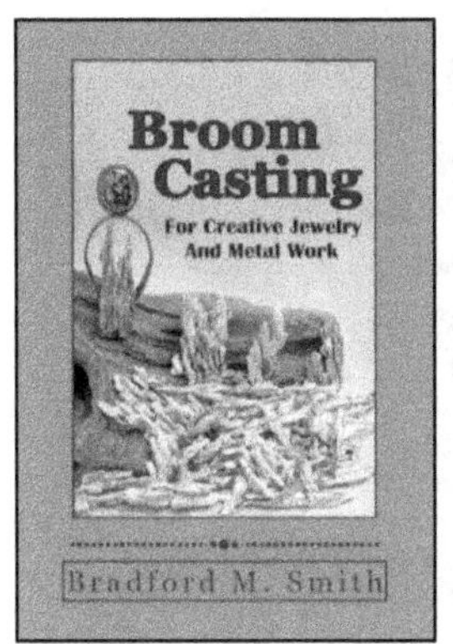

Discover the rush of pouring molten silver into a straw broom to get marvelous icicle-like shapes that just beg to be designed into finished jewelry like pendants and earrings.

Broom casting is a technique that yields beautiful results, doesn't require a lot of time to learn, and is just plain fun to do. In a couple hours you can be producing intriguing geometries that spark the imagination and challenge your creativity.

"Broom Casting For Creative Jewelry" gives step-by-step procedures for casting and covers proper use of all equipment. It includes how to work with the irregular shapes for your designs and has suggestions for safety, tips for cleaning & polishing, and ideas for making some of your own tools. Other sections cover how to run your own broom casting workshop for friends & club members and a gallery of finished jewelry utilizing some of the cast shapes.

amazon.com/dp/0988285835/

Amazon Reader Reviews

- I've found Broom Casting a little intimidated, but I love the look. So I was really excited to hear about this book. Brad Smith's book really takes the mystery out of the process. He breaks down the steps really well, and walks you through the process clearly and simply. Then he shows you how to look at, clean/cut, and finally create with the castings. He really covers this cool technique from top to bottom. It's all in this great little book.

- Broom Casting for Creative Jewelry and Metal Work outlines everything you need to know to start and continue broom casting silver.

More Bench Tips For Jewelry Making

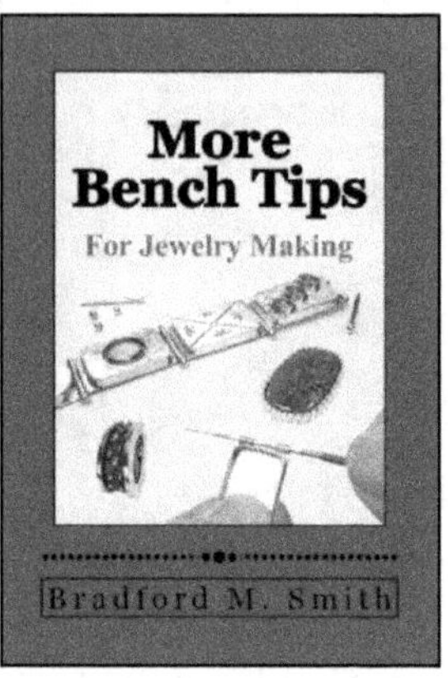

In every field top artisans have favorite ways of solving common problems. Making a piece of jewelry is no exception. Accomplished jewelers have shortcuts and special tools to help them save time and increase the quality of the work.

This second volume of Bench Tips includes 86 ways to save time, avoid frustration or improve quality in areas of fabrication, stone setting, casting, soldering, and polishing.

These tips from the author's extensive shop experience will help you get the most out of your tools, keep costs under control, and avoid common hazards. "More Bench Tips" is written as a resource for jewelers with skill levels from beginner through advanced.

amazon.com/dp/ 0988285886/

Amazon Reader Reviews

- Easy to understand writing style, clear and concise instructions. Absolute MUST have for any artisan -- beginner and advanced alike.

- This is my third book from this author. Very informative and nice techniques are mentioned in this book. What I like is these information does not overlap with my other books. I got much more than what I paid for this book! No doubt 5 stars.

- I own and treasure the first book, Bench Tips. This is a great sequel to that book. Very good tips and useful information for the beginner and advanced metalsmith.

Accessories for the Foredom and Dremel

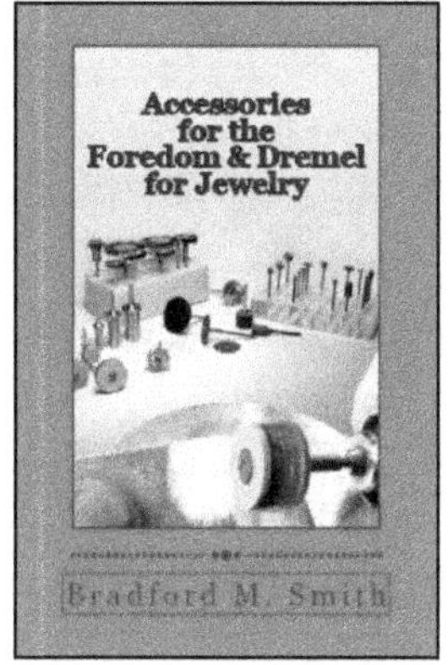

Flexible shaft and Dremels are an indispensable help to those who make jewelry, improving both the productivity and the quality of work. But with such an array of different tool bits to choose from, it's sometimes difficult to figure out which bits to use.

"Accessories for the Foredom and Dremel" surveys the range of tool bits available for use with flexible shaft and hand-held motor tools and discusses the merits of each.

It highlights the best drill bits to use, the three most useful cutting burs, six different types of sanding bits, five ways to polish your work with the Foredom or Dremel, and five bits that can be used to add texture. In each category, I share my experience with the tool bits which save the most time, mention bench tips for getting the best results, and add cautions for safe use.

amazon.com/dp/0988285878/

Amazon Reader Review

- Five Stars - What a little treasure! … This book, while small, is packed full of great information on the subject. It's a great resource to keep handy at your bench.

The Reluctant Farmer of Whimsey Hill - A Memoir

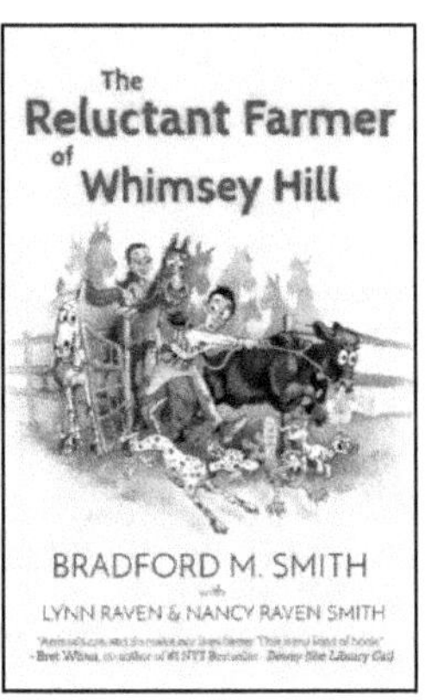

The Reluctant Farmer of Whimsey Hill is a light-hearted, true love story between more than a man and a woman. Imagine *Marley and Me*, not with one pesky dog, but with a farm full of quirky animals.

The narrative follows Brad's fish-out-of-water point of view as a 25-year-old, animal-phobic, computer nerd from the city who moves to a rural, Virginia farm with his new, animal-loving bride. There he's propelled on a journey of self-discovery as his bride's crazy animals teach him about life and love - the hard way.

amazon.com/dp/0988285851/

Editorial Reviews

- Animals can and do make our lives better. This is my kind of book.

  - Bret Witter, #1 NYT bestseller co-author of Dewey [the Library Cat]

- A witty memoir reminding us that the best lessons in life are beyond the edge of one's comfort zone, and one can only be towed there by the heart strings."

  - Jean Abernethy, creator of Fergus the Horse

Amazon Reader Reviews

- Anyone who loves animals, has a sense of humor and appreciates a good, clean book (plenty of mud though) will love this book!

- A charming, witty, well written account of the country life of a young couple, with some sweet moments and some laugh out loud moments. We thoroughly enjoyed it.

www.ingramcontent.com/pod-product-compliance
Lightning Source LLC
LaVergne TN
LVHW010543100826
845148LV00013B/2574

* 9 7 9 8 9 8 7 3 9 1 5 0 1 *